CCW Graduate School | RGAP 2013

Rebecca Fortnum

Kate Hawkins

Marc Hulson

Jim Threapleton

Marius Von Brasch

Beth Harland

Donal Moloney

Nina Pancheva-Kirkova

Lindsey Adams

Paul Goodfellow

Johanna Love

Rachel Sharp

Behind the Eyes
Making Pictures

Edited by Beth Harland

Exhibition: Gallery North, Northumbria University
24 January–3 March 2013; Symposium: 25 January 2013
Curated and edited by Beth Harland

Photography: Beth Harland's paintings Alick Cotterill;
sources of Rachel Sharp's paintings Brandon Stanton;
Marc Hulson's paintings Digitalarte.

ISBN 978-0-9569024-7-4
All rights reserved
Copyright © 2013 the authors
Designed by Colin Sackett
Printed and bound in the U.K.

RGAP (Research Group for Artists Publications)
www.rgap.co.uk

CCW Graduate School
16 John Islip Street, London SW1P 4JU

Distributed by Cornerhouse Publications
70 Oxford Street, Manchester M1 5NH
www.cornerhouse.org

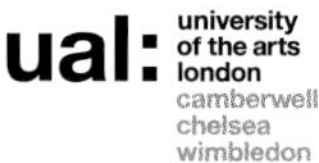
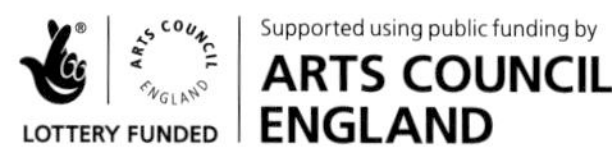
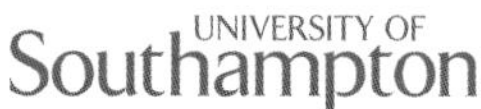
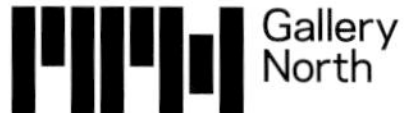

Preface

The relationship of painting and drawing to photography has been much explored and discussed, with the claim sometimes made that a *re-working* of an indexical image trace, through material process, sets up a productive space of 'removal'. This project, which encompasses an exhibition, a symposium and the current book, comes out of an interest in returning to the notion of re-working, or *re-seeing* an initial source image in the context of recent pictorial practice. The aim is to explore the distinction between capturing appearance, which might be very immediate, a moment: an *image*, and something that is 'constructed', involving another duration entirely: a *picture*.

In looking for something 'other' than the initial recorded image, the artists involved in *Behind the Eyes: Making Pictures* necessarily engage, in their own terms, with the terrains of image and picture, and with the dialogue and difference between them. They establish strategies of making which become individualized forms of mediation, articulated at times with reference to notions developed elsewhere such as 'trait', 'Becoming', and 'looking away'; or describe their making through terms such as 'supplemental', 're-inscription', 'concealment' and 'de-composition'.

The exhibition, held at Gallery North, Newcastle-upon-Tyne, presented works by Lindsey Adams, Rebecca Fortnum, Beth Harland, Marc Hulson and Johanna Love. It included forms of documentation alongside completed works, to explore some of the usually tacit aspects of artistic process in the dialogue between image source and picture-making. The symposium presented papers by early-career researchers from Winchester School of Art,

University of Southampton: Marius von Brasch, Kate Hawkins and Nina Pancheva-Kirkova; from CCW Graduate School, University of The Arts, London: Donal Moloney and Jim Threapleton; and from Northumbria University: Paul Goodfellow and Rachel Sharp.

Material from both the exhibition and the symposium are represented here in edited form.

Beth Harland, May 2013

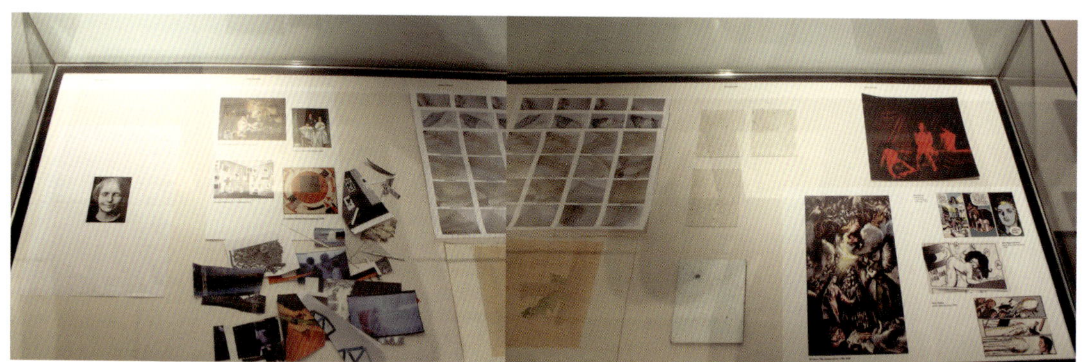

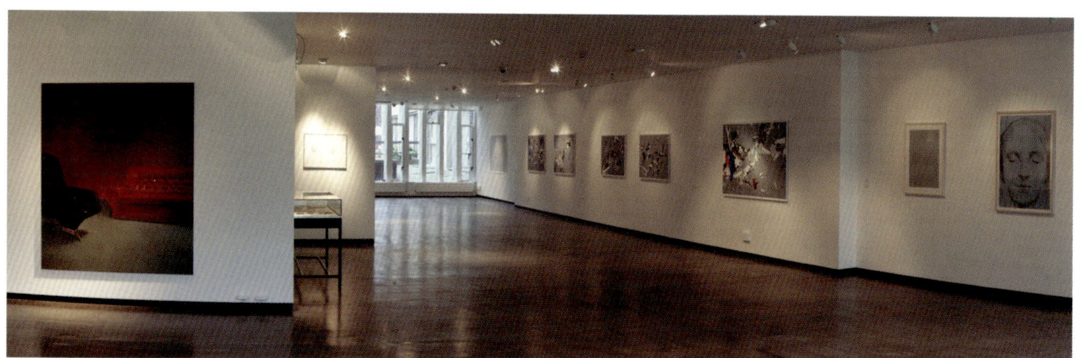

ABOVE: Behind the Eyes: Making Pictures, exhibition display of artists' sources
BELOW: Exhibition, installation view

BETH HARLAND

Introduction

"A good picture, which is a faithful equivalent of the dream which has begotten it, should be brought into being like a world." (Baudelaire, *The Salon of 1859*)

Though it precedes his more frequently quoted characterisation of an admirable picture, in *The Painter of Modern Life,* Baudelaire's notion of painting *as world* somehow extends it. In the *Modern Life* text of 1863, his call to artists is to capture the moment at its most fleeting and contingent, while equally achieving a timeless quality—the fugitive being just "the half of art whose other half is the eternal and the immutable" (Baudelaire, 1995: 13). However, the *Salon* text already brings us to the heart of his expectation that a painting, as well as addressing 'modernity', should be more than an image of something in the world; it should attest also to the imagination, and more emphatically still, to "the *constructive* imagination", which he considers a "higher function" (Baudelaire, 1965: 159 italic in original). He underlines this further by likening nature, for an artist, to a dictionary, pointing out that "no one has ever thought of his dictionary as a *composition*, in the poetic sense of the word" (Baudelaire, 1965: 159–60 italic in original), and declaring that those who lack imagination can do no more than reproduce the dictionary through simple copying.

The artist's 'dictionary' (and perhaps with it, the 'imagination' in some sense), has undergone a radical transformation since the 19th Century, and the current equivalent of the painting of modern life must steer a course through a somewhat bewildering array of new and reinvented entries. While the dictionary evolves, and the workings of the imagination strive to keep pace, there is something compelling and precise in

Baudelaire's vision of the picture's world which seems a useful model for the thinking that picture-making involves, now as then. After all, there may be nothing new for an artist in the fact that picturing one's times involves complex, intertwined questions, both of *what* is pictured and *how*. Baudelaire's text engages with ideas of what it means to compose, to build a picture, opening onto a rich territory of image transformation, mediation, distance and temporality—central concerns within much current pictorial practice. Hal Foster touches upon these questions in his review of the exhibition *The Painting of Modern Life*, and describes painting as "…a resemblance to the world that is less direct, more mediated by material, touch and tradition." He points to the importance of painting's temporality, the fact that it tends to take time to produce and also to view, in establishing what he sees as its fundamental assets: "its remove and its delay" (Foster, 2007).

Jean-François Chevrier, in a recent seminar series on the history and discourse of pictorial composition and the *tableau,* explored the complex distinction between image and picture, noting that the English term *picture* is close to, though not quite the same as, the French *tableau* (Chevrier, 2012). He insists that a picture is not an image: it is something more than an image; it has another dimension. An image can be reproducible, an 'instantaneous composition', a form of seeing that does not involve picture-making, and does not have the picture's autonomy as an object. Of course, in these terms, a photograph can be either an image or a picture, and Chevrier specifically situates his discourse beyond medium. Similarly, the current project is not a debate about the medium of painting, or drawing; rather, its focus is upon how these pictorial practices might seek something 'other' than the initial appearance of an image source, something that is, as the title has it, *behind the eyes*.

Through processes of re-imagining and the materiality of their practices, the artists here enter the territory evoked by Jean-François Lyotard in his description of Cezanne's endeavour: "to make seen what makes one see, and not what is visible" (Lyotard, 1991: 102). These practices invoke sensation, affect, and the act of looking itself. The work of picture-making involves a second approach to an initial idea or trace, and in the process of approaching again, different elements and qualities enter the space. Perhaps we might say, at the level of the image, something else gets in.

And so to Baudelaire's 'constructive imagination': I want to ask what it is and how it might operate in the work of artists engaged in pictorial practice. There is clearly a process of mediation, the object of 'painting as world' is not simply a view *of* the world, but something that is built out from that first image; it becomes more psychological than geographic. The picture of constructive imagination is a pictorial unity of the conceptual and the material; not a picture as *window*. In a discussion between Chevrier and Jeff Wall in 1990, Wall describes the importance of achieving a "dramatic mediation of the conceptual element…", which links with previous statements he has made about achieving pictorial unity in which he references Baudelaire's emphasis on construction in picture making. Wall states that, without this process of mediation: "images become a decorative completion of an already fully evolved thought. They are just illustrations." (Wall, 1996: 104)

Here an understanding of tableau becomes useful. As Chevrier presents it, the relationship between picture and tableau is complex: they are linked, but not directly equivalent. While a tableau can be an easel painting, or a photograph, neither of these forms necessarily have all of the characteristics to qualify as one. A tableau is a plane; an object; autonomous and 'limited', and, importantly, is presented to the viewer in a particular way. Chevrier tells us the experience of looking is upright and "confrontational". The distinction between image and picture is reiterated: the picture is more of an object than

is an image, hence closer to tableau. And he says: "Tableau has nothing to do with image." (Chevrier, 2012)

A tableau, then, combines elements, in some sense *frames* them, and is a holder of complexity. Similarly, 'constructive imagination' might be described as the combination of *image* and *composition as a process*, which brings about a productive space of mediation. It might also imply the bringing together of an external view and an internal, subjective experience, in the world of the picture. This is reminiscent of Proust's exquisite description of his character Marcel's encounter with the blurring of perceptual boundaries:

Upon the sort of screen mottled with different states and impressions which my consciousness would simultaneously unfold while I was reading and which ranged from the most deeply hidden aspirations of my heart to the wholly external view of the horizon spread out before my eyes at the bottom of the garden… (Proust, vol 1: 90)

In this passage, we 'see' the multiple, layered construction of temporality at the heart of Proust's remarkable novel, itself a theory of knowledge. The link between this and Baudelaire's description of the creation of the picture's world seems clear: it is a world characterised as 'thick' with layers of time, all of which are present in the finished composition.

But, to add to this layering, we should include the viewer, in whose mind the parts of a picture are put together. In a sense, the world of the picture must account for that which is outside itself. A supreme example of a composition which operates according to this principle is Velazquez's *Las Meninas*, a painting whose pictorial strategy incorporates the space of the viewer by moving beyond its frame to that which is outside its own field of view. The complexity of this work's address to the viewer, and of its temporal implications, distinguishes it from the realm of image; its very construction generates a forceful and particular space that is able to encompass the field of the viewer, and the painting as world.

Baudelaire's calls for a constructive imagination is a call not just for skills but for *ideas*, and an alertness to one's time, combined

with imagination. This is why it has continuing
and compelling relevance for current pictorial
practice. The reworking of pictorial ideas
and structures continues, whether it be to
address familiar motifs in a different mode,
or to incorporate developments in technology
and spectatorship into a traditional form; the
discourse of images and pictures remains active.
Chevrier's call, in his seminar to an audience
largely made up of young artists, was for a return
to the problems and challenges of composition,
of the tableau, within a contemporary context. In
a time of ever-increasing access to image sources
and forms of production, and with, perhaps
as a result, a greater need to be clear about the
continuing ambitions of pictorial practice, such
a call is a stimulating and exacting challenge.

References

BAUDELAIRE, C. (1965) *Art in Paris 1845–1862; Reviews of
Salons and Other Exhibitions*, London: Phaidon

BAUDELAIRE, C. (1995) *The Painter of Modern Life and
Other Essays*, London: Phaidon Press

CHEVRIER, J-F. (2011) *The Tableau Form: Methodology and
Composition*, Seminar, Central Saint Martin's College of Art,
London. Part of the *Tableau Project* led by Mick Finch

FOSTER, H. (2007) 'At the Hayward', *London Review of
Books*, vol.29, no.21

PROUST, M. (1983) *Remembrance of Things Past*, London:
Penguin Books

LYOTARD, J-F. (1991) *The Inhuman*, Cambridge: Polity
Press

WALL, J. (1996) 'The Interiorized Academy', interview with
Jean-François Chevrier 1990, in *Jeff Wall*, London: Phaidon

Rebecca Fortnum is a London-based artist and
Reader in Fine Art at CCW Graduate School,
University of the Arts, London.

Kate Hawkins is a PhD candidate at Winchester
School of Art, University of Southampton.

Marc Hulson is a London-based artist and a
founder member of the London based artists'
co-operative Five Years.

Jim Threapleton is a PhD candidate at CCW
Graduate School, University of the Arts, London.

constructive imagination | image and composition | picture/ tableau | complex acts | transformation | modified | bricolage | hinge | re-seeing | emerging double | latent content | extraction | construction | permutations | plasticity | model | interwoven | materiality | aura | entropy | performative | tenor | cognition | subjectivities | absorbing | fragmentation | oscillate | layers | topology | gist | mediation | echo | de-composition | sideways | distraction | temporality | performative | supplemental | quotation | metanarrative | resonance | symbiotic | technology | image search | interactive | capture | system | simulating | strategies | looking away | supplement | becoming | destruction | fragment | superformula | reference | re-inscription | chance | marking | shadow | hybridise | dissociation | decipher | re-reading

Rebecca Fortnum | Kate Hawkins | Marc Hulson | Jim Threapleton
Marius Von Brasch | Beth Harland | Donal Moloney | Nina Pancheva-Kirkova
Lindsey Adams | Paul Goodfellow | Johanna Love | Rachel Sharp

REBECCA FORTNUM

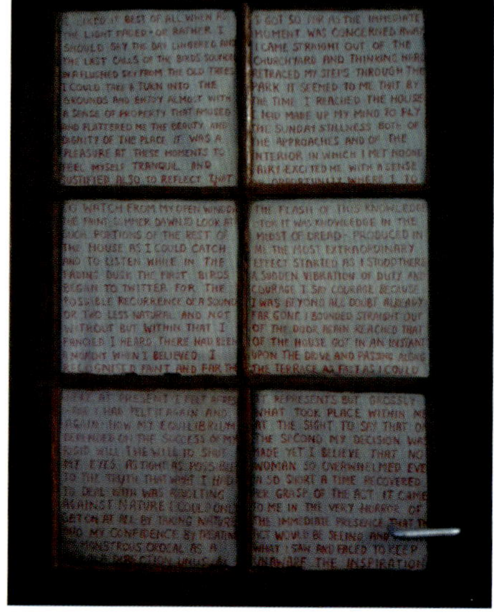

possible to the truth that what I had to deal with was, revoltingly, against nature. I could only get on at all by taking "nature" into my confidence and my account, by treating my monstrous ordeal as a push in a direction unusual, of course, and unpleasant, but demanding, after all, for a fair front, only another turn of the screw of ordinary human virtue. No attempt, nonetheless, could well require more tact than just this attempt to supply, one's self, *all* the nature. How could I put even a little of that article into a suppression of reference to what had occurred? How, on the other hand, could I make reference without a new plunge into the hideous obscure? Well, a sort of answer, after a time, had come to me, and it was so far confirmed as that I was met, incontestably, by the quickened vision of what was rare in my little companion. It was indeed as if he had found even now—as he had so often found at lessons—still some other delicate way to ease me off. Wasn't there light in the fact which, as we shared our solitude, broke out with a specious glitter it had never yet quite worn?— the fact that (opportunity aiding, precious opportunity which had now

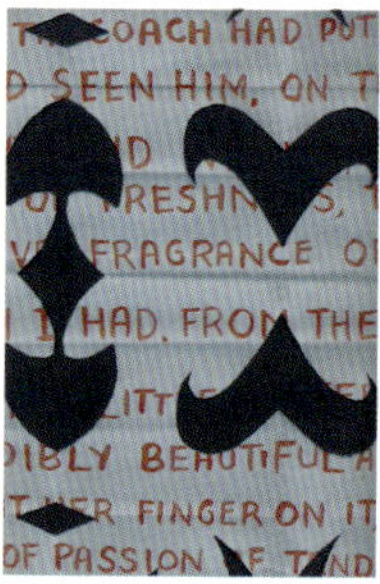

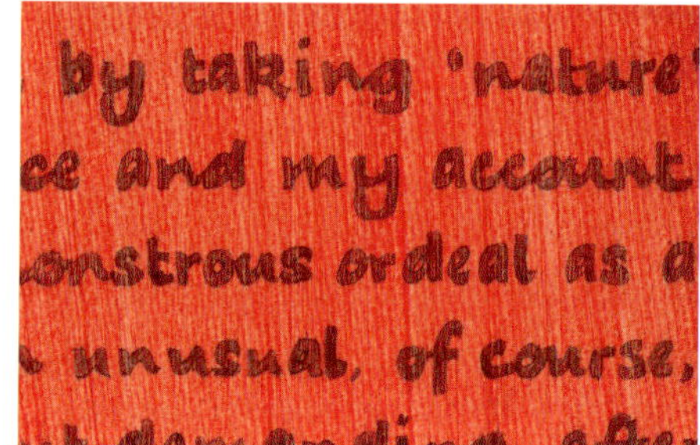

In 2011, when undertaking a research project *Drawing in—and outside—Writing*, I began to examine the power the activity of reading held for me. I understood that I was most interested in text and image as sites of return and that my method would revolve around re-drawing images and re-reading narratives. For me reading is a way to create a hiatus or a disruption of the linear progression of time. For a while I can enter into a different pace of things. I had read *The Turn of the Screw* by Henry James, a story that exists within a dense web of interpretation, before— more than once. I came to be curious about the how the protagonist, the childrens' governess, tells her story, using self-narration as an act of self-determination, a weapon to battle her sense of pervading stasis or even oncoming oblivion. She makes herself by telling her tale.

For a while I have been returning to an image too. *The L'Inconnue de la Seine,* has provoked stories that interweave fact and fiction, her image is embedded in words. In responding to her image my drawing functions as an act of resuscitation; the figure is revived by the movements of the pencil—literally drawn back to life—referencing L'Inconnue's contemporary reincarnation as *Rescue Annie*. With these drawings I continue to re-visit the image; the task of the drawing never seems complete. I am looking for a way of making a mark that is somewhat mechanical and devoid of the autograph but I suppose I am also hoping that, in this re-iteration, something else might arrive on the paper, a certain quality that is always just out of reach. This extended process of copying attempts to neutralize the expressive mark and to make this more explicit I have shown these drawings as paired portraits. I am interested in how we 'read' images comparatively; when a drawn face is copied an other emerges, neither an individual nor yet quite a clone and,

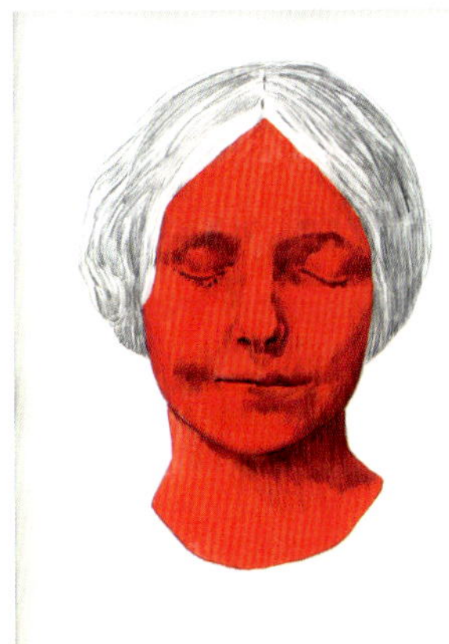
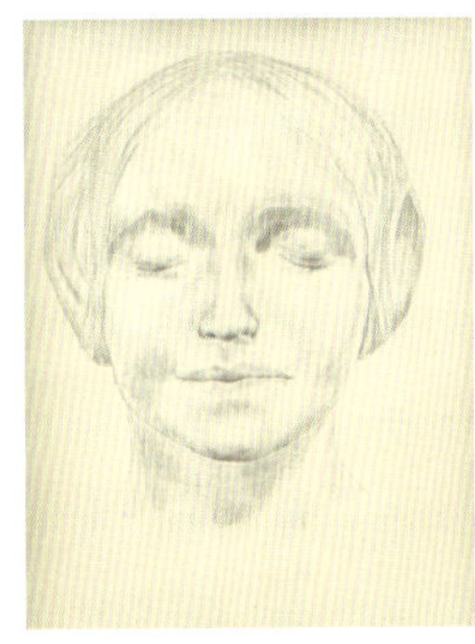
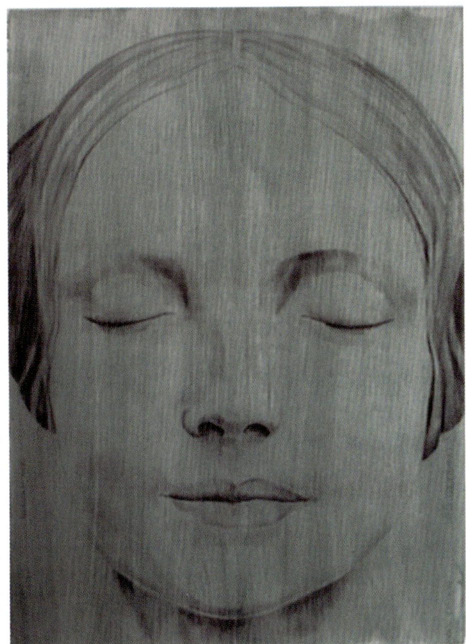
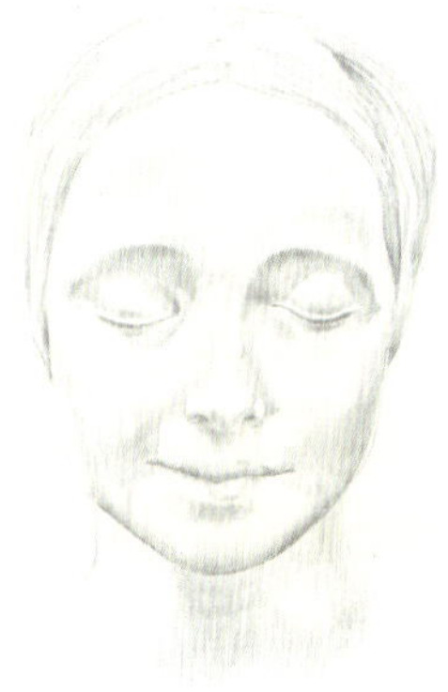

for me, provides a sense of provisional or unstable identity. It also acknowledges the submerged yet insistent notion of 'reading' a countenance.

Eventually the governess's self narration attached itself irredeemably to the image of the unknown girl who was pulled, drowned, from the banks of the Seine probably around ten years before James' story was published in 1898. It was only later that I discovered L'Inconnue had already been paired with the story's other (spectral) governess by Maurice Blanchot, as he attempts to describe the tone of poetry in his essay *A Voice From Elsewhere*. Here the L'Inconnue—whom he encounters as a death mask on his bedroom wall —and Miss Jessel, the former governess now dead, become emblematic of an immaterial presence, offering us, like poetry, access to an untranslatable 'otherness', beguiling yet impossible to fully articulate.

The difficulty of this attempt to describe the elusive 'voice' of literature might be compared to the draughtsman's task. How to draw has long occupied me. By this I don't mean what 'style' to employ (although that is in itself an interesting issue) but rather how to deal with the impossibility of drawing from looking; what mental and dexterous conjuring is required in the translation from sight to mark. In *Memoirs of the Blind* Derrida describes the problem:

> *How can one claim to look at both a model and the lines that one jealously dedicates with one's own hand to the thing itself? Doesn't one have to be blind to one or the other? Doesn't one always have to be content with the memory of the other?* (Derrida, 1993: 36)

The draughtsman cannot simultaneously draw and look and he cannot see his drawing as he draws. In my drawings this act of memory— the space of translation—is examined through

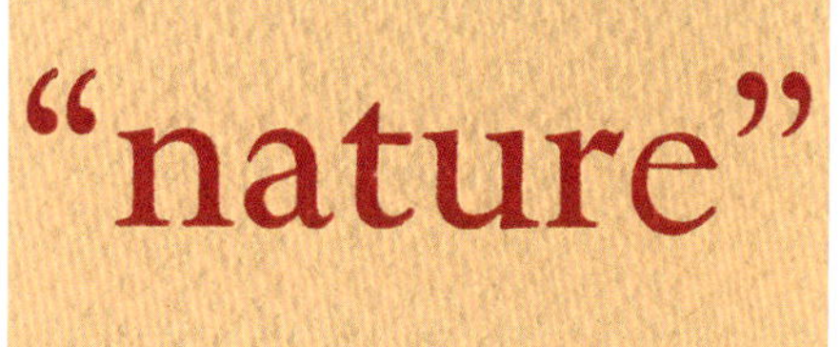

"nature"

here at present I felt afresh - for I had felt it again and again - how my equilibrium depended on the success of my rigid will. I could only get on at all by taking "nature" into my confidence and my account, by treating my monstrous ordeal as a push in a direction unusual, of course, and unpleasant, but demanding, after all, for a fair front, only another turn of the

different processes of ma(r)king. Within a pair the first drawing memory is often squeezed by technology, with the projector or tracing paper stepping in for the sun in Butades' indexical process, yet in the subsequent drawing it becomes the core of the process, both haptic and optic memory forced into play to recreate the image. I am interested in the work's second hand value as 'mere copies' (as Derrida termed the drawings his brother made from family photographs). For Derrida the traits (mark, trace, line) of the drawing are followed by the retrait or withdrawal, the "differential inappearance of the trait". I understand this as that which occurs as the beholder (artist and spectator alike) makes sense of the drawn image. Derrida explains how the drawing's line marks only the "single edge of a contour" so in order to see the image the viewer must, necessarily, conjure into the drawing's image that which is absent thus abnegating the trace itself. The inadequacy of the trait, in this respect its confinement to the

contour, explained my interest in the use of cross hatching and led me to understand my desire to make drawings only of vertical lines of varying lengths, suggestive of early computer drawings using binary code. Yet I found that at points of emphasis (indeed of crucial differentiation between different surfaces or planes) I fell back upon the horizontal mark. I was not machine enough to avoid it completely. In the two images side by side (trait and retrait) even small shifts in the lines' placement and length can create the curious paradox of dissimilar twins.

To counterbalance his brother's proficiency with images Derrida becomes a master of "that accord of time and voice that is called (the) word", which he thinks of as a "substitution" for drawing, a "trait for a trait". For him this is an exchange, one or the other and, indeed, using both image and text is perhaps tautologous. But the text remained, and eventually, after an attempt to embed excerpted passages in my surroundings, I selected some that chart the governess' attempt

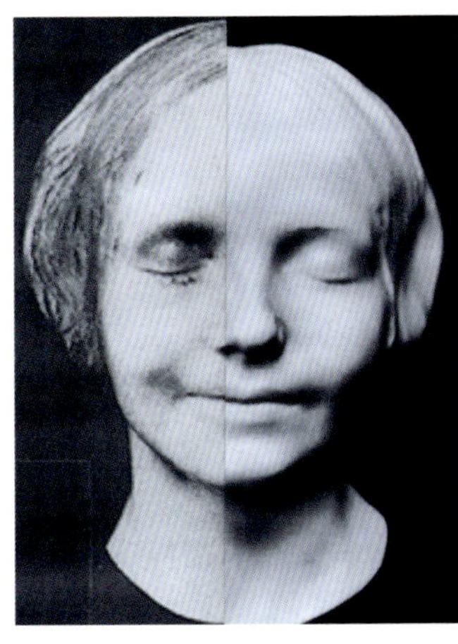 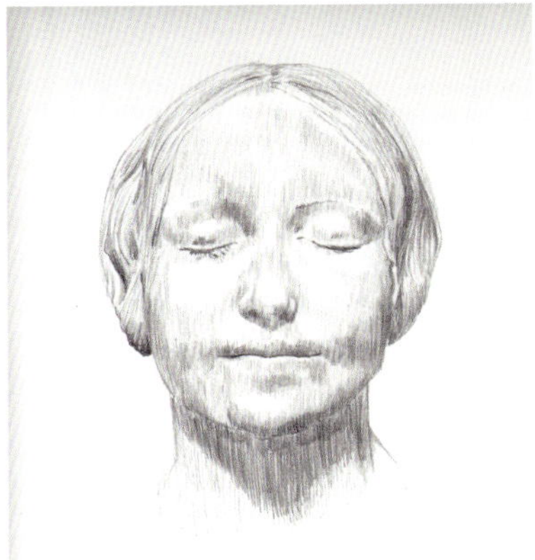 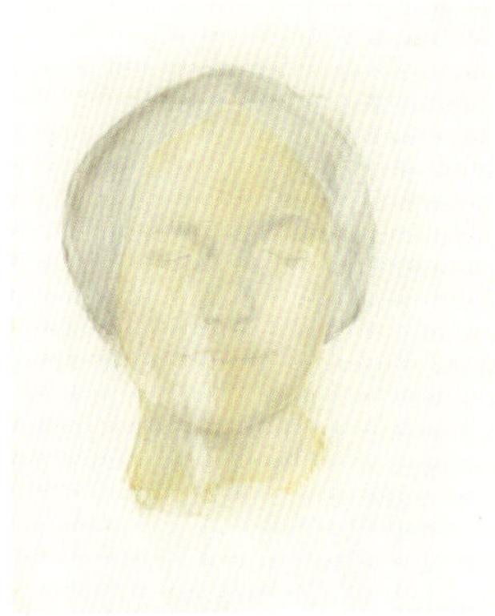

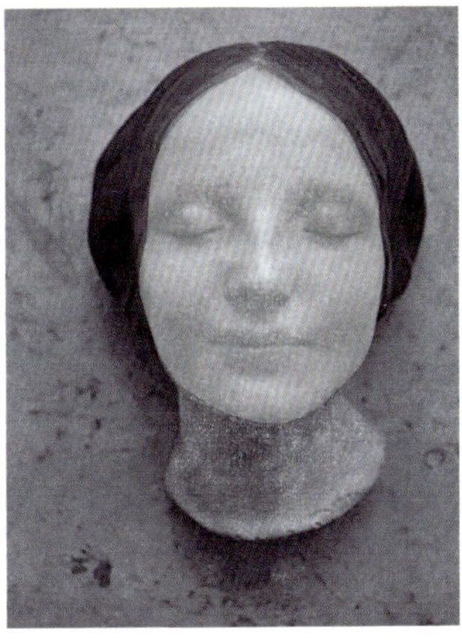

to govern herself. Marooned from their story these pathetic word gatherings cease to carry their narrative thrust and instead linger painfully "sublime within simplicity". They materialized as handset letterpress works in Perpetua font which, predating the digital age, are themselves hand drawn. For me the imprints of these letters represent the perfection that the drawings themselves continue to fall short of. Together with the L'Inconnue drawings, text and image, they became *In a flushed sky* that formed the resolution of my project.

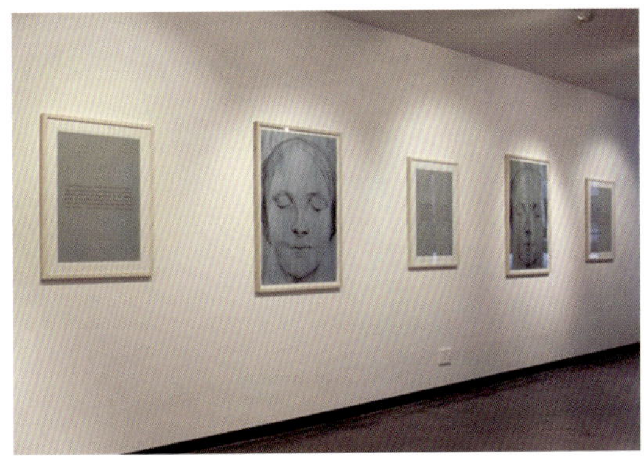

References

BLANCHOT, M. (2007) *A Voice from Elsewhere*, first published 2002, translated by Charlotte Mandell, New York: SUNY Press

DERRIDA, J. (1993) *Memoirs of the Blind: the Self Portrait and Other Ruins*, Chicago & London: University of Chicago Press

A full version of this essay can be found in the cahier, *Drawing—in and outside—Writing* published in 2012 by Uitgeverij Acco.

KATE HAWKINS

'Looking Away' From The Stage

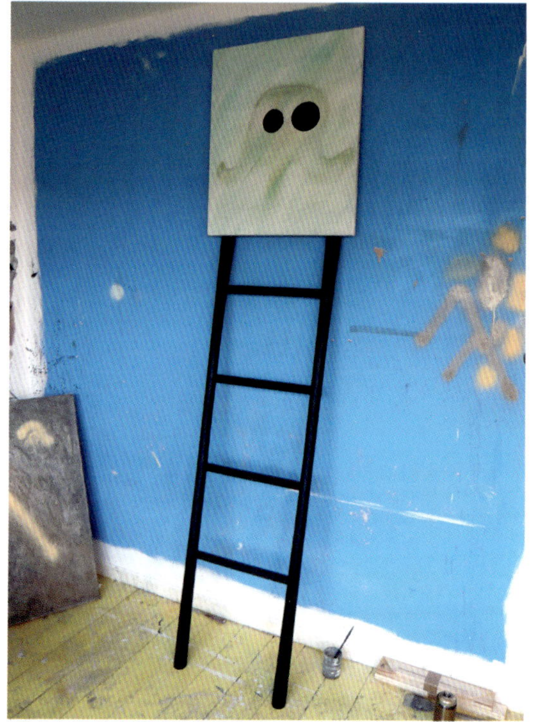

Studio shot, 2012

In her text *Looking Away: Participations in Visual Culture,* Irit Rogoff explains how through "looking away" in a gallery context, "we produce for ourselves an alternative mode of taking part in culture… that break(s) down the dichotomies of objects and viewers"(Rogoff, 2005: 133). She goes on to explain that through this series of performative acts "audiences shift themselves from being *viewers* to *participants*"(Rogoff, 2005: 122).

In my own studio practice I also 'look away' and often consciously hide the digital images I employ as source material from view while painting. I use such images widely but always in manipulated, changed states preferring to re-make, or re-see them. I never work directly from photographs—the act of looking or absorbing the image in front of me is always interrupted, most often by the physical act of looking away from a printed image, or of closing my laptop so that I can no longer see an image on the screen.

The Physical Act of 'Looking Away' in the Studio

I. ACTION

'Looking away' in the studio necessitates a physical movement from the artist, which in turn 'activates' a dynamism in the work. In the same way that Jackson Pollock's dripped and splattered canvases expressed energy, emotion, process and psychological freedom, the action of 'looking' and sometimes 'moving' away from my source material brings another, if simpler, physical energy to the work. It could be argued that even a simple physical movement such as 'looking away' can

help free and loosen an artist into producing more open-minded, unbound and uncontrived works. According to Jean-Paul Sartre, freedom is existence, and in it "existence precedes essence", (Sartre, 1946: 27) implying that what we do, how we act in our life, determines our apparent 'qualities'. It is not that someone tells the truth because she is honest, but rather she defines herself as honest by telling the truth again and again. Essentially our *acts* define us.

Harold Rosenburg writes of Action Painting: "At a certain moment the canvas began to appear to one American painter after another as an arena in which to act… What was to go on the canvas was not a picture but an event."(Rosenburg, 1952: 22) The 'act' of painting became the 'work' as opposed to the 'work' symbolizing the 'act'.

II. DISTRACTION

The physical act of 'looking away' breaks the attention span bringing about a distraction. The study below links distraction, which Rogoff talks of in a gallery context, to something like a science of intuition. In the same way that Rogoff views distraction positively, encouraging performative acts to occur in traditionally sober gallery spaces, Ap Dijksterhuis revealed that distraction can help us make better (complex) decisions. In 2006 he asked study subjects to evaluate four models of cars based on twelve variables. Dijksterhuis found that only about twenty-five percent of those who were given uninterrupted time to ponder their choice opted for the best model, compared with sixty percent of people who were asked to make a decision after looking over the cars and while performing another task. "While they were focusing on something else, the unconscious mind was processing the information and integrating it into a valid selection" (Dijksterhuis, 2006) he explains, concluding that complex decisions are best made after a period of distraction assumed to elicit unconscious thought.

Dijksterhuis' *Unconscious Thought Theory* hypothesises that unconscious thought (deliberation without attention) is better for making complex decisions where there are many variables in play whereas conscious thought is better for simple decisions with fewer variables. I would reason that 'painting' is a process with many variables i.e. complex, therefore requiring unconscious thought for better decisions and that my strongest paintings result when those decisions are made quickly on something akin to an unconscious level. The painting *Two Moustaches* was made exceptionally quickly and intuitively, in roughly two minutes, yet is, for me, one of my stronger works.

III. VULNERABILITY

The physical act of 'looking away' from my source material in the studio makes me 'blind' and vulnerable as an artist and encourages me to rely much more on my inner reserves and intuition by removing the 'scaffolding' of the photograph. In this way the making becomes less of a transmission of the image already in existence and more of a means of constructing something new.

On the surface, vulnerability and courage seem like a contradiction in terms, but Brené Brown concludes, after twelve years of research, that vulnerability is our most accurate measurement of courage: "vulnerability is the birthplace of innovation, creativity and change… to create is

Paint and Screws on Studio Wall, 2012
Digital inkjet on archival paper, 42 x 29 cm, ed. of 50

to make something that has never existed before —there is nothing more vulnerable than that." (Brown, 2012) Correspondingly, I would argue it is the physical act of 'looking away' in the studio that allows for vulnerability, and perhaps even encourages it, enhancing creativity in the process. Ultimately Brown argues it is vulnerability that paves the way to authenticity.

The Performative Act of 'Looking Away' in the Studio

It is authenticity that I would like to explore in relation to performativity versus theatricality, rooted in the act of 'looking away'. Rogoff explains how through the performative gesture of 'looking away' conscious and contrived connections are disrupted in favour of new and innovative avenues. In my practice, the act of 'looking away' from my source material encourages performativity steering me clear of making theatrical and overly conscious artworks. For example, *Paint and Screws on Studio Wall*, actively encourages a consciousness of viewing. At first glance it appears as a face yet on closer inspection it is simply a studio wall with some wonky screws.

Michael Fried's argument is that theatricality, not performativity, results from a disruption to the viewing process; a painting is theatrical when it provokes a certain consciousness of viewing and the spectator is interrupted from (optimal) self-transcendence. Although both Rogoff and Fried see theatricality, in relation to the viewing of artworks, negatively, they understand disruption of viewing in opposite ways. Fried believes that interruption to the viewing process disrupts absorption and is more likely to result in theatricality. Contrastingly Rogoff regards disruption of viewing positively because of its potential to promote performativity.

In the following extract by Rogoff, an exhibition viewing was 'unframed' from its mythic structures because of two disrupted viewing positions. Yet promisingly Rogoff and G.B. walked out of the exhibition being able to tell *both* stories in which they had *both* participated:

> *G.B. and I have gone to see the Jackson Pollock exhibition at the Tate Gallery, London… Shortly after entering the exhibition… we spot the actress who plays the beautiful nurse Carol Hathaway in the fabled TV series ER. We are mesmerized, we follow her around the exhibition… Our attention has been well and truly diverted and one mythic structure—the heroic modernist figure of Pollock and the art history that instates him—has been interrupted by another mythic structure, that of Hollywood celebrity. [Furthermore] a viewing position, an alternate of imbricated fan as opposed to reverential spectator, was put into play in this disruption.* (Rogoff, 2005: 129–130)

This seems to me to be what 'looking away' in the studio does[1]—it allows you to communicate *both* as artist and spectator. It enables participation simultaneously within two identities, two mythic structures. Also in 'looking away' while painting I give myself the power to unframe my studio from its own mythic structure and initiate a performative. This performative means that something gets done, artworks get made. Further-more the *action* triggered by the physical process of looking away frees me to make better work; the *disruption* inherent in the act of looking away stimulates intuition, while the *vulnerability* felt by looking away promotes authenticity. I hope by 'looking away' in the studio to make freer, more intuitive and more honest work.

1. By using the word 'does' here I am alluding to Dorothea von Hantlemann's performative text 'How To Do Things With Art', and also J. L. Austin's definition of the performative which states that in any performative utterance (or speech act) the sentence actually does something as opposed to describing something being done. For example: I *bequeath* this watch to my sister or I *pronounce* you man and wife.

References

BROWN, B. (2010) *The Power of Vulnerability* [online] available at http://www.ted.com/talks/brene_brown_on_vulnerability.html TED [accessed on 21 January 2013]

BROWN, B. (2012) *Listening to shame* [online] available at http://www.ted.com/talks/brene_brown_listening_to_shame.html TED [accessed on 21 January 2013]

DIJKSTERHUIS, A., BOS M. W., NORDGREN, L. F. & VAN BAAREN, R. B. (2006) 'On Making the Right Choice: The Deliberation-Without-Attention Effect' in *Science*, 17 February 2006: 311 (5763), 1005–1007. [DOI:10.1126/science.1121629]

FRIED, M. (1988) *Absorption and Theatricality: Painting in the Age of Diderot.* Chicago: University of Chicago Press

POLLOCK, J. (1947) *My Painting in Possibilities.* I. Winter 1947–48. pp. 78–83. New York: Wittenborn, Schultz, Inc.

ROGOFF, I. (2005) 'Looking Away: Participations in Visual Culture', in *After Criticism: New Responses to Art and Performance.* ed. G. Butt. Oxford: Blackwell Publishing

ROSENBURG, H. (1952) 'The American Action Painters' in *Art News* 51/8, Dec. 1952, p.22

SARTRE, J-P. (1948) *Existentialism and Humanism.* tr. Philip Mairet 1973 ed. London: Methuen

VOSS, J. L. & PALLER, K. A. (2009) 'An Electrophysiological Signature of Unconscious Recognition Memory' in *Nature Neuroscience*, DOI: 10.1038/nn.2260

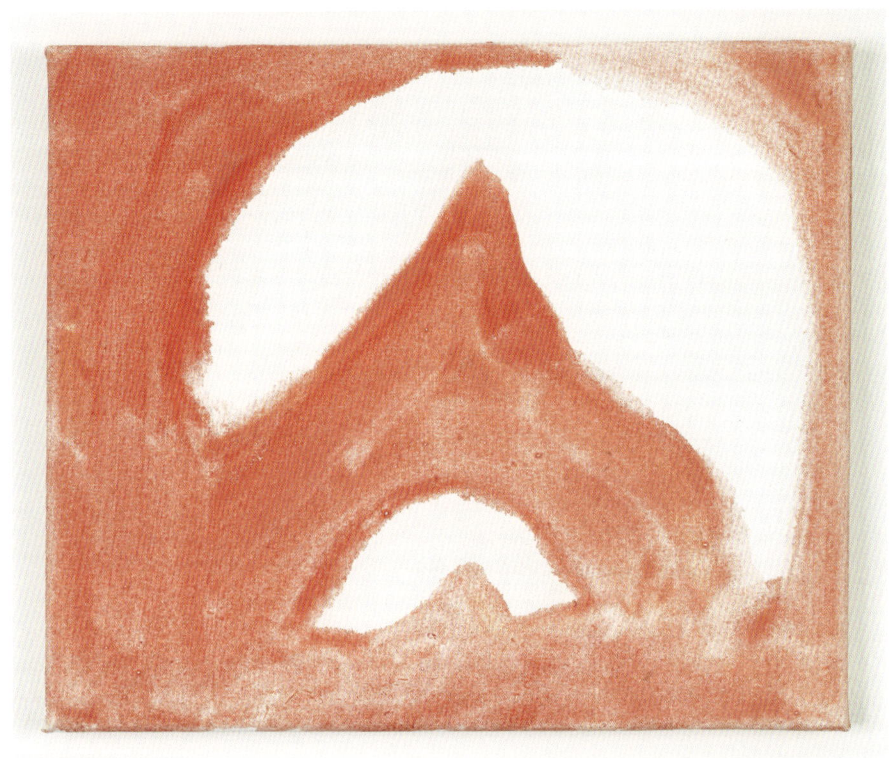

ABOVE: *Two Moustache*, 2012, Oil on canvas, 31 x 35.5cm
BELOW: *Two Black Marks On Mirror*, 2012, acrylic on mirror, 32.3 x 49cm

MARC HULSON

The figures in my paintings and drawings are occupants of a quasi-theatrical pictorial space. Often ambiguous in gender, masked or subject to physical distortions and deformations, they inhabit an indeterminate fictional milieu that continually subdivides as it evolves.

While working I often hybridise multiple sources, including studies from life, my own photographs, found images and, to a large extent, the 'imagination', a resource which I don't really distinguish from 'memory': a mosaic or cuttings folder of mental snapshots taken from remembered perceptual experience, dreams and images remembered from a multiverse of external media. As such the imagination is an important reservoir of information for me, and it engenders a kind of freedom—not as an arena for self-expression, rather as a sort of common ground, like a street or a tip that can be trawled for detritus, found material, buried treasure. The bodies in my work are formed from these fragments, as is the body of work as a whole.

As a general rule I start with an idea in physical or mental sketch form and proceed by gathering whatever information is appropriate or necessary to the evolution of that particular idea. This doesn't involve any consistent or systematic relationship to source material: sometimes an encounter with a particular image, or the memory of such an encounter, triggers possibilities in my work; sometimes I seek out source images and make preliminary studies relevant to what I'm working on; while other paintings and drawings are worked to completion without any direct reference to an external source. There's no consistent external factor, but I do continually refer back in some sense to previous works of my own, so there's an internal chain of repetition, transformation and consequence or reference that functions as one of the main drives.

The figures in the works included here are all loosely based on sets of drawings and photographs from a model made in 1999 and 2000. One set was taken by me in the studio, with source material for paintings in mind, and was highly staged. Another—from the same model but more spontaneously executed—was given to me by the artist Esther Planas.

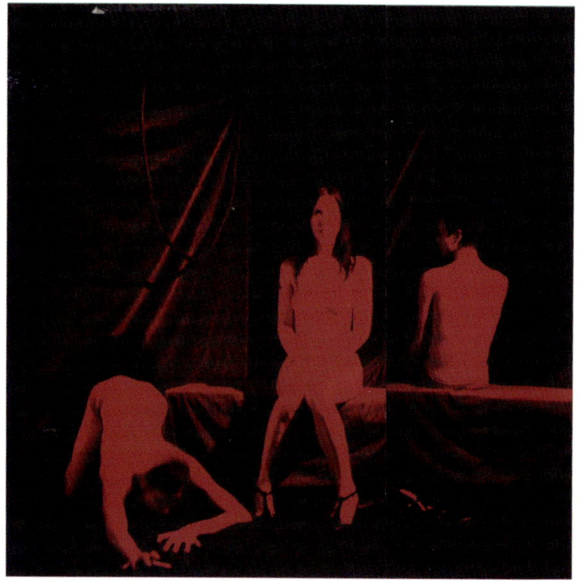

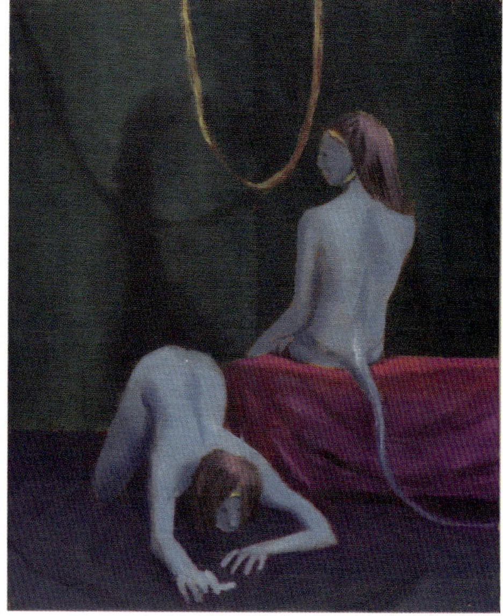

Studies for *Theatre Facsimile*

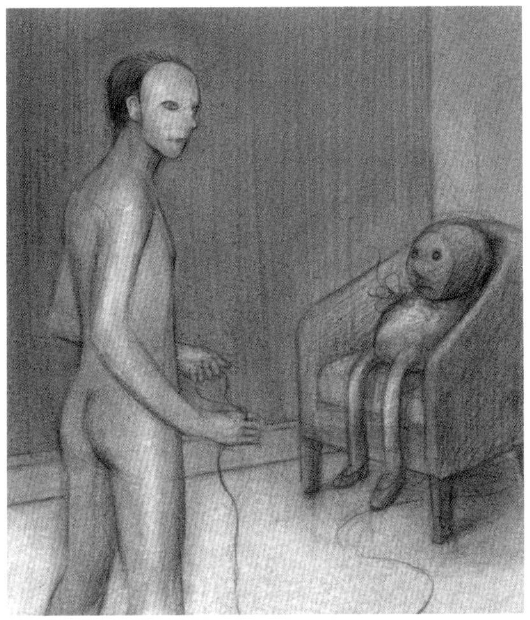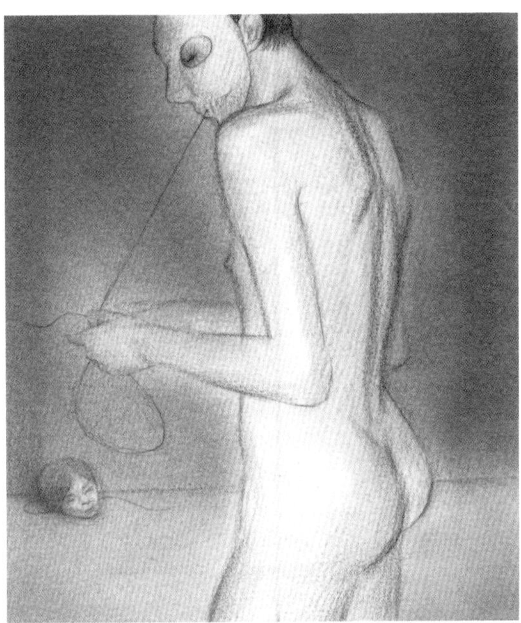

Untitled 2011, each 18 x 15cm graphite on paper (from the series *Cast* 1998–2013 / ongoing)

The working materials represented in this publication include the original studio photographs mentioned above, which relate directly to the painting *Theatre Facsimile*. I had used coloured filters on the camera lens to distance the shot from reality, interfering at the point of source with the image's status as a document or source of precise local information. I made numerous further prints that were collaged and drawn over as preliminaries to the painting, as well as compositional and colour studies in oil and pastel as the work developed.

At the same time, the palette, composition and poses were influenced tangentially through encounters with various works by other artists between 1999–2005. In 2002 my first significant experience of El Greco's works, in particular the extreme stylizations of form, colour and the abstraction of corporeality in his large scale *Annunciation* at The Prado in Madrid, had a lasting impact. Work by Jose Miguel Alvarez, Steve Dillon and Paul Gillon in the graphic novels *ChiChi Squad*, *Preacher* and *Les Naufrages du Temps* also influenced the evolving language of my work at the time.

Sometimes the image that resolves a particular work occurs to me quite unexpectedly, and is incorporated towards the end of its development. Ultimately each picture emerges intuitively, through crystallisation—the process of editing and condensing whatever raw material I'm working with through the medium itself, feeling my way toward a particular mood or atmosphere, seemingly dictated by touch, surface, materiality and the formal parameters of the pictorial field.

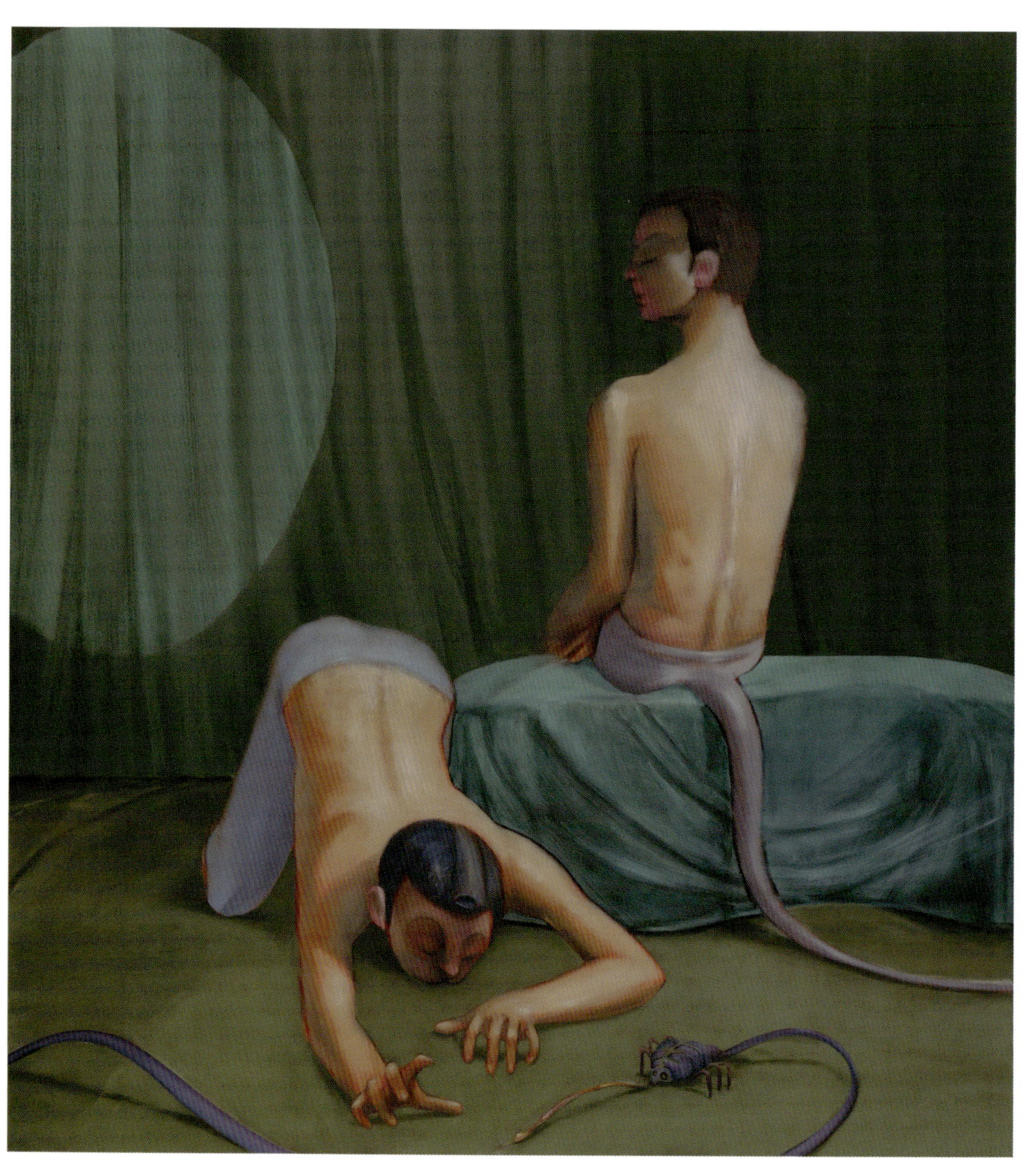

Theatre Facsimile, 2006, oil on canvas, 171.5 x 152.5cm

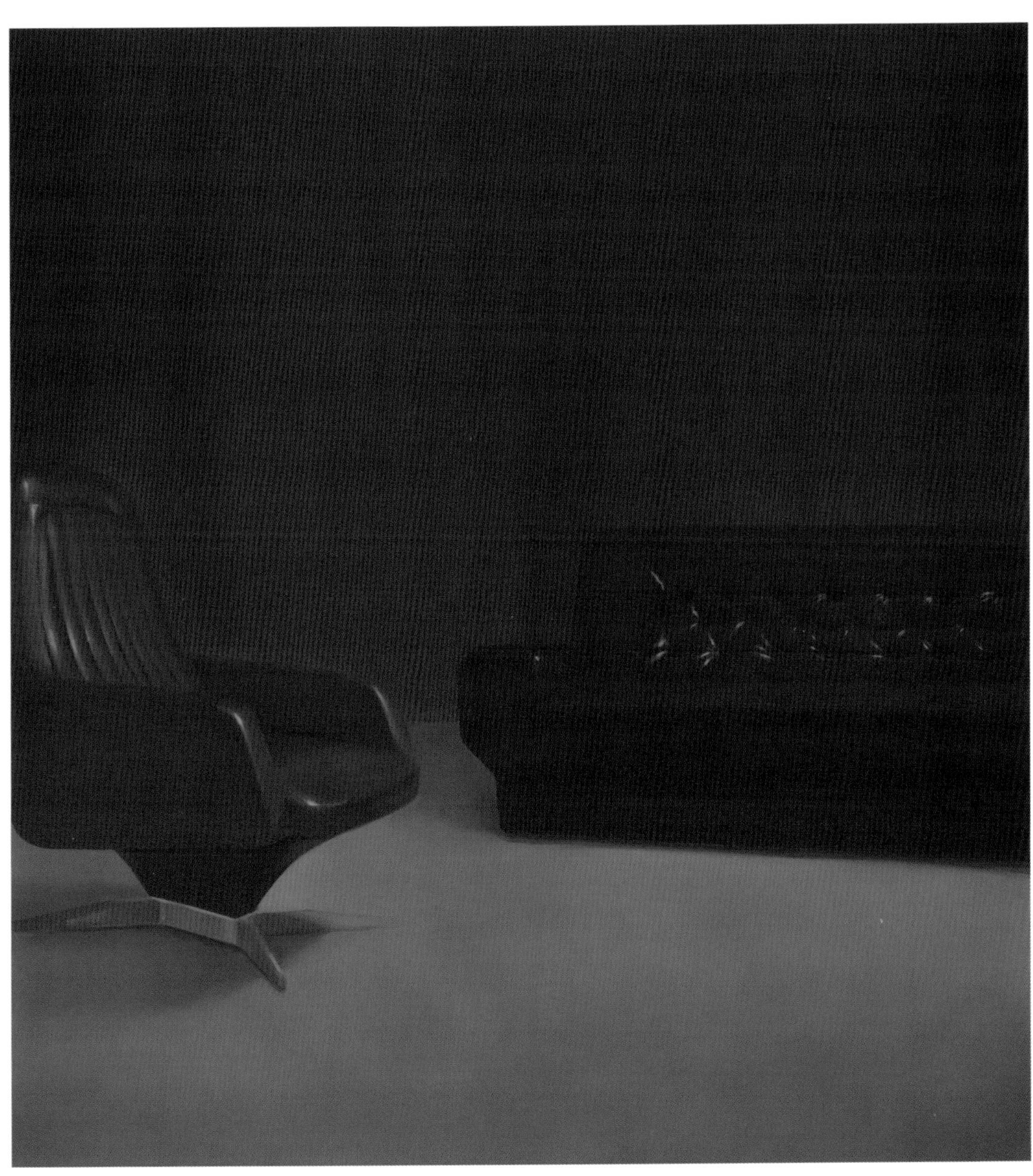

L'invitation, 2010, oil on linen, 180 x 160cm

JIM THREAPLETON

The Corroded Surface: Portrait of Entropy (De-composition as a means to a pictorial end)

For me the relationship between image [source] and work is defined by an orientation towards the negative, towards what Samuel Beckett described as impoverishment, a lack of knowledge; towards subtracting rather than adding. Reduction serves the pursuit of image in nascent or provisional state, found at the porous boundary between representation and abstraction (Schwabsky, 2011:14–15). The process of making a picture is invariably foreshadowed by the stultifying question of where to begin. Perhaps channeling Beckett, François Lyotard associates this anxiety with waiting, he situates it in the traumatic possibility of nothing happening—not just at the beginning of a work but at each point of questioning, at every turn that asks: "and what now?" (Lyotard, 1988, Morley, 2011: 29). Long since stripped of academic, religious or illustrative agenda, painting and the pictorial, like Beckett's characters Estragon and Vladimir in *Waiting for Godot*, have been left wandering the postmodern limbo of worn out essentialism, the one crying "we're saved!" before the other declares "nothing to be done" in the face of the absurdity of articulating the un-presentable.

To complicate matters further, as Gilles Deleuze points out, the canvas is never actually empty, it is already "invested with all kinds of clichés which the painter will have to break with" (Deleuze, 2003: 8). The break is violent. The

relationship between image source and final work, between faithfully recorded photographic fact and pictorial truth is essentially an antagonistic one. For Deleuze the painter "…paints on images that are already there, in order to produce a canvas whose functioning will reverse the relations between model and copy." (Deleuze, 2003: 8).

This reversal is activated by material process. The action of painting provokes a transition between states, from solid to air—from the concrete (typically photographic) artifact, universal and loaded with association, de-sensitized through re-reproduction across an infinite digital landscape, to the prototype—or painted work—particular, unique, something wholly other, with an autonomy and truth.

Driving this movement between states is a downward, vulgarizing, entropic force. This is the dismantling blast of Bataille's *Informe*, the performative operation that levels hierarchies, liberating visual form from ontology. Image is brought closer to the state of idea through corruption and debasement. Dragged away from the literal, source material is savaged. Picture making in these terms is a destructive business. Images are harvested, cut, cropped, blown-up, erased, violated; the painted surface is smeared, scored, and scraped to a point of indeterminacy and a state of abjection. Subjectivity propels the work back and forth between past and

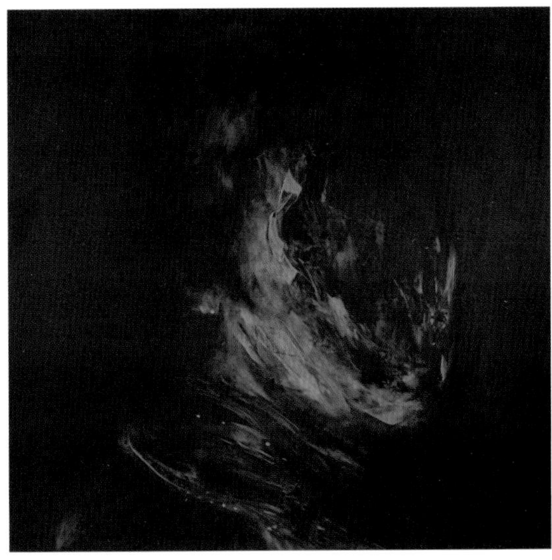

Bis 2-chlorethyl sulfide VI, 2012
Oil on stainless steel, 100 x 100 cm

future tense, between its pictorial origins and its aspirational presence.

When Deleuze wrote his text on the work of Francis Bacon he surely could not have predicted just how besieged by image and cliché the post-modern painter would become in the age of photoshop, instagram and google images, where ever-splintering culture is determined by citation and irony, privileging pastiche over authenticity. An endlessly updating, unfiltered stream of traffic means that image is no longer captured it is unavoidable. Instead it is the pictorial that must be worked for. Material process provides the conditions to capture the electrical pulse discharged between opposing poles—whole/fragment, figure/ground, control/accident, form/formlessness, presence/absence and image/picture.

The malerisch tearing open of imagery drives the viewer from image to surface, from the optic to the haptic—from seeing to feeling. This is the romance of painting. The evocation of a vocabulary associated with post-Kantian notions of the ineffable is deliberate. As Lyotard points out, despite a rejection of the eloquence of Romantic Art, it remained the case that picture making in the modern period and beyond has remained faithful to the "fundamental task of bearing pictorial or otherwise expressive witness to the inexpressible" (Lyotard, 1988, Morley, 2011: 30).

The black monochrome has served as scaffold for my basic interest in how paint moves. The particular fluidity of oil paint, its unpredictable kinetic potential is intrinsic to my exploration of painting as a negative language—negative, that is, in the most positive sense. Composition is revealed through de-composition. Sensation is favored over sense data. Source material is subjected to brutish processing. Methods that, in some ways, add up to sculptural process reduce the work to the binary—zero or one, paint or no paint, mark or non-mark, depth or flatness.

My work is defined by the navigation of a tipping point that Francis Bacon described as the "complete interlocking of image and paint, so that the image is the paint and vice versa" (Bacon, 1953: 12). This point of indeterminacy, where a fleeting relationship between marks made communicates image, articulates feeling and divests resonance. The portrait is presented as missing contents. The figure is a subjective, repressed, residual presence carried in the accidental smear of rag, the cata-strophic drag of a finger or the erasing scythe of the brush.

Making pictures is a process of synthesis, of drawing together the distinct but nevertheless complimentary languages of the theoretical and the practical, of critical thinking and thinking in paint. Sources are not limited to imagery. Collaged with the outwardly visible there is the shape-shifting 'image' of the sublime. The surface is

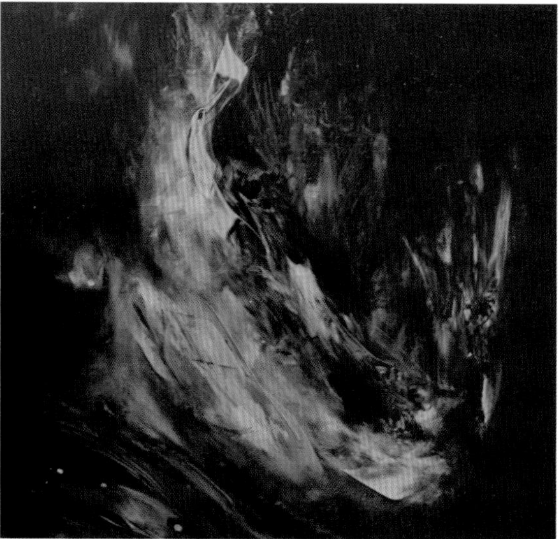

Bis 2-Chlorethyl sulfide VI (detail), 2012
Oil on stainless steel, 100 x 100 cm

also clogged with the paint of my influences—the gestures, tics and techniques borrowed, stolen and co-opted from a rich and intimidating genealogy.

Picture making is discovery; the action of painting embodies research. My practice has traced a shift from photographic sources to reproductions of paintings. By drawing directly on historical referents, principally the work of Rembrandt, a dialogue is initiated that photography simply cannot contribute to. More than mere citation, Richard Kendall describes Leon Kossoff's direct use of Poussin's paintings as a mean of penetrating a little into their identity and finding structures of his own to account for their success. The resulting work is a distinct act of creation, self-sufficient and autonomous. For Kendall this type of symbiotic relationship between a work and its direct antecedents attests to the "creative co-existence of the studio and the museum" (Kendall, 2000: 32).

My painting is determined by the decisions that arise in the making. Mark and gesture guide intuition. Compositional tension is generated from how paint is physically put down, or rather taken away. Working repeatedly from a single source, image as such becomes a given, leaving an unresolved set of variations that become a kind of contradictory proposition of negation in painting encountered as an accumulated experience. There is no intermediate state between source and work.

No preparatory studies prescribe how much of the source material will endure. The study is in the progression of image, or the image of painterly progression. The subtractive mark is a kind of hole within the whole, a void within unity. The unfinished or barely started quality of the painting articulates the impossibility of presentation or representation, the implausibility of satisfaction in expression. Invariably, pictorial structure is born of the frustration of articulation, of my limits as a painter. It proceeds from backward steps in the painting, from the cancelling out. Passages of smeared paint appear stable and affirmative before they melt away into negative space. The violent tracings of dragged paint form phrases of a cursive script of sorts that testifies to the trauma of process.

References

SCHWABSKY, B. (2011) *Vitamin P2*, London: Phaidon

LYOTARD, F. (1988) 'The Sublime and the Avant Garde' in Morley, S., 2010, *The Sublime*, London: Whitechapel/MIT Press

DELEUZE, G. (2003) (Eng transl.) *Francis Bacon: The Logic of Sensation*, 3rd ed, London: Continuum

BACON, F. (1953) *Matthew Smith: Paintings from 1909–1952*, London: Tate

KENDALL, R. (2000) *Drawn to painting: Leon Kossoff drawings and prints after Nicolas Poussin*, London: Merrell

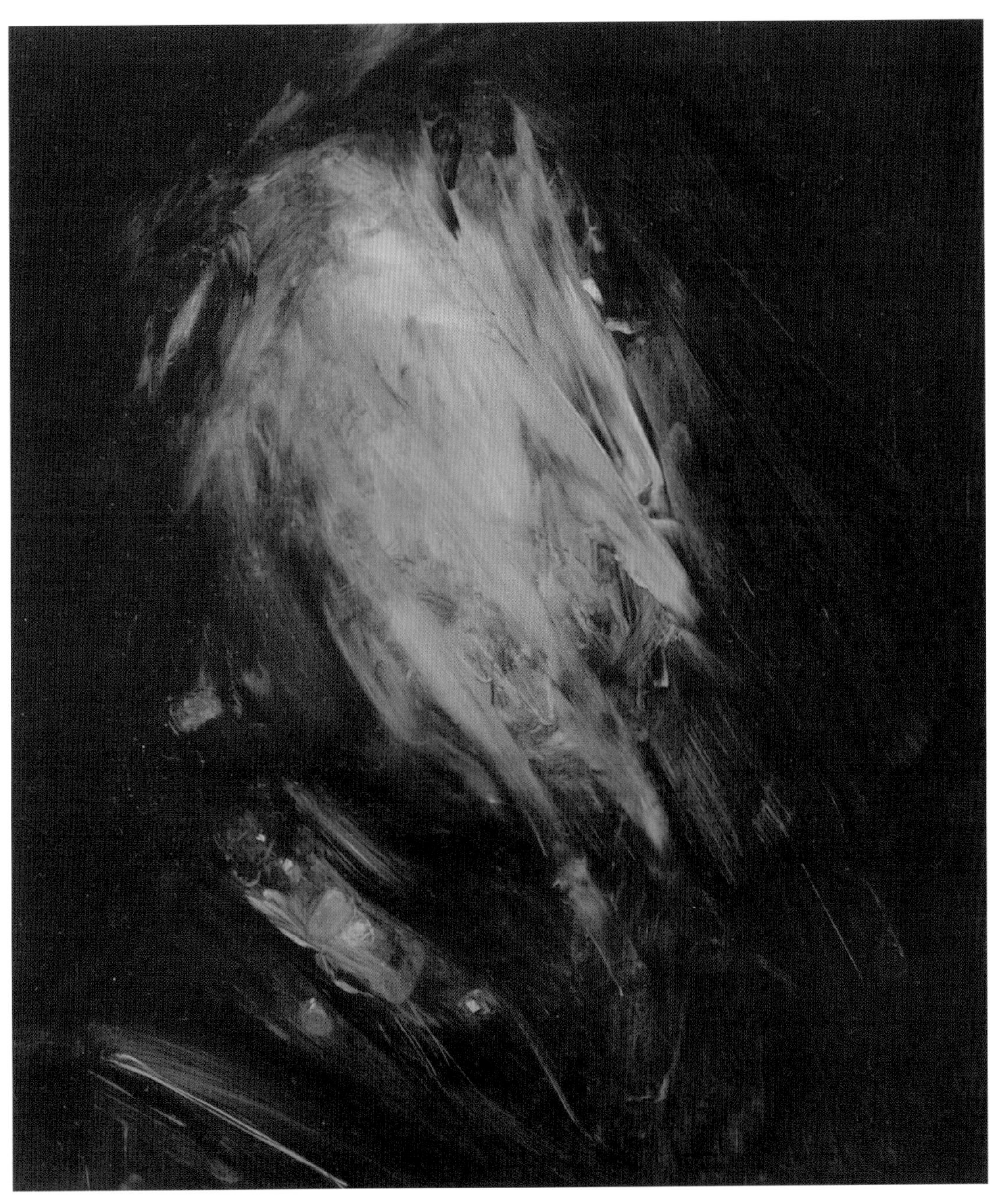

Loss of Other Modalities of Sensation XV, 2012
Oil on stainless steel, 40 x 30 cm

Marius von Brasch recently completed a PhD
at Winchester School of Art, University of
Southampton.

Beth Harland is a London-based artist and
Reader in Fine Art and Head of Research Degrees
at Winchester School of Art, University of
Southampton.

Donal Moloney is a PhD candidate at CCW
Graduate School, University of the Arts, London.

Nina-Pancheva-Kirkova is a PhD candidate
at Winchester School of Art, University of
Southampton.

constructive imagination | image and composition | picture/ tableau | complex acts | transformation | modified | bricolage | hinge | re-seeing | emerging double | latent content | extraction | construction | permutations | plasticity | model | interwoven | materiality | aura | entropy | performative | tenor | cognition | subjectivities | absorbing | fragmentation | oscillate | layers | topology | gist | mediation | echo | de-composition | sideways | distraction | temporality | performative | supplemental | quotation | metanarrative | resonance | symbiotic | technology | image search | interactive | capture | system | simulating | strategies | looking away | supplement | becoming | destruction | fragment | superformula | reference | re-inscription | chance | marking | shadow | hybridise | dissociation | decipher | re-reading

Rebecca Fortnum | Kate Hawkins | Marc Hulson | Jim Threapleton

Marius Von Brasch | Beth Harland | Donal Moloney | Nina Pancheva-Kirkova

Lindsey Adams | Paul Goodfellow | Johanna Love | Rachel Sharp

MARIUS VON BRASCH

Affective Constructions: Fragmented Images on the Axis between Painting and the Digital

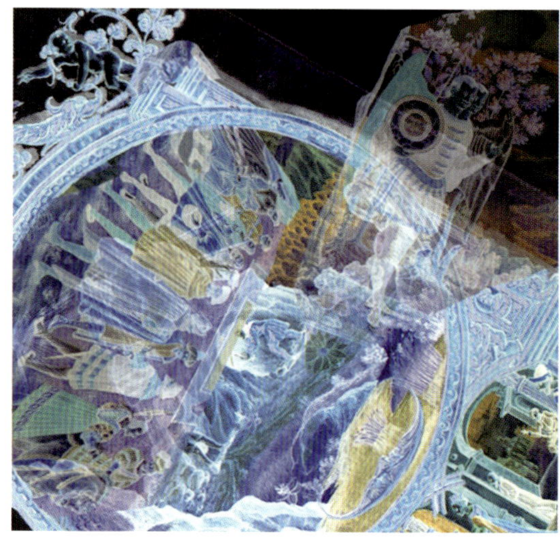

This text responds to the project by discussing the role of source images in my practice-based research, which proposes new ways of visualizing and conceptualizing the notion of *aura* in art, understood as an affective sensation experienced in intuitive art practice and the encounter with art.

As a notion, *aura* became important in critical theory through Walter Benjamin's seminal essay from the late 1930s, *The Work of Art in the Age of Its Reproducibility* (Benjamin 2002), where he targeted *aura* as the link between contemplative religious modes and the aesthetically staged rituals of fascist politics. The sensation that the *experience* of *aura* tries to capture, as he writes it, is a "strange tissue of space and time: the unique appearance of a distance, however near it may be" (Benjamin 2002, 104) pointing at both, historical and subjective, strands. Benjamin hoped technologies of reproduction and dispersion would challenge the 'original' and 'authentic' and thus liberate collective creativity to free 'play'— outside of religious origins and against capitalist strategies. However, *aura*'s desired decay remains in his (materialist) Marxist critique also hinged to the hope for Messianic (thus transcendent) intervention.

My research (Von Brasch 2012) set out to test whether there could be a potential of a conception of *profaned aura*, one that would acknowledge its presence in intuitive art practice and own it

for experimental use without having to return to religious or psychological 'origins'.

The departure point became the question of what *aura* could mean for painting in an expanded field, especially in relation to digital imaging.

Foregoing a need to bind phenomena (and art practice) back to first causes opens exploring their becoming within temporality, their dynamic potential and incessant being-in-change. Becoming different from themselves with every moment, 'things' and practices reveal more of their temporal thresholds when they are without definable beginnings or ends than when static 'objectivity' submits them to control. From this perspective—inspired by Gilles Deleuze's concept of *Becoming*, which is central to his endeavour to think metaphysics outside of fixed thought images—art practice embodies a "veritable theatre of metamorphoses and permutations" (Deleuze 2004a: 68), beyond the restricted drama of subjectivity. It opens towards and touches affects (rather than personal affections) and percepts (rather than mere perceptions).

Aura, in this framework, appears as a conduit for affects as it is involved with a sensitivity for the dynamics of the unresolved; of questions and those spontaneous 'events', which like dice-throws emerge from virtual (in the sense of not yet lived) potential and intensities in linear time. Far from being "illusion" or "a beam of the original" (Mosès

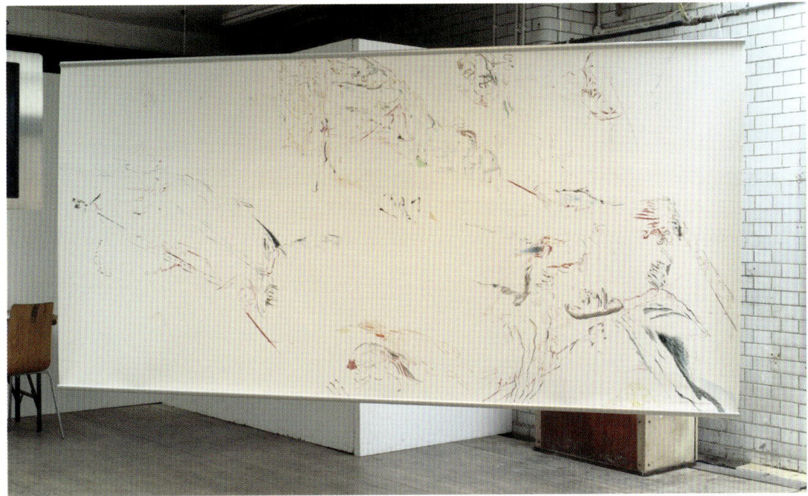

2009: 78), *aura* connects to *Becoming* like an 'echo'.

The practice contextualized and juxtaposed this aspect with source pictures that deal with *images* of *aura* literally and developed strategies of mapping minor, less obvious strands of *aura*. The basic aspect of the practice element—intuitive or 'chaotic' mark making, extending to painting and video—seemed to be mirrored by Arnaud Villani's demand for "complex acts": "*letting* oneself act", "to let the virtual infuse, without forcing it" (Villani 2010: 77).

Major visual sources were Mathis Grünewald's *Resurrection* (completed 1515) and *Splendor Solis* (from about 1600)[1]. In the latter the successions of the alchemical Great Work (presented in 22 images) culminate in an *image* of *aura*, a vanishing point where 'opposites' to be united disprove their 'binarity'. However, as all 22 frames interact throughout the work as thresholds of *Becoming-aura*, *aura* always already interweaves, a fusion of dark and light, *all* the frames and transformations of the series.

The practice involved projections of digital fragments or composites of source images onto paper or canvas, thus temporary, digitally mutable *images*: all are based on photographs functioning originally as documentation of artworks, which are scanned, processed, projected. During the process of making, these unstable images are further moved, modified, zoomed, rotated, inverted, following both impulses and conceptual considerations; their 'work' in between things and eyes evokes how ancient writer Lucretius envisions them "perpetually / Flowing and falling from things and moving away", "[f]or there is always something streaming off / From the surface of things which they eject. And this, / When it meets some things passes through them, like glass" (from Book 4 of Lucretius 1999: 105).

In this sense, the outcomes—holding the transitory images and their "positive power which denies *the original and the copy, the model and the reproduction*" (Deleuze 2004b, 299)—are constructed of shards of different times, affective responses and potential future-Becomings. Like crystals, they contain "the present [as] the actual, and *its* contemporaneous past" (Deleuze 2008a: 76) and yet exist as material and tactile composites, evoking what Beth Harland calls "haptic time", "a time without entry or exit" privileging "material presence over representational structure" (Harland 2009: 66).

Enabling more fluency than analogue collage, technology is used in this research for production and the 'materiality' it offers; used with an awareness that it is not 'neutral', and with a focus on not forgetting/denying the 'complex act', on practising a mode of absorption in letting oneself be traversed.

Mapping along the axis between painting and digital input concerned foremost finding and *inventing* those lines of flight, which destabilize the metaphysics of representation developed in (thought) *images* of *aura*. However, inviting unpredictable complexity and *a-subjective* forces meant also taking the risk of experiences, which relate to a caesura, a mark of the potential loss of the constructed self, of intensities that triggered what Deleuze calls a "wound that existed before me" (Deleuze 2001: 31).

How could this 'wound before me' have relevance for the practice element?

A wound encountered in this research—while working on *diversely streaming* (2011), a set of three large drawings involving fragments of Grünewald's *Resurrection*—became a gradual and very unexpected return of sorrow about friends I have lost to Aids nearly twenty years ago. This personal wound proves to be one that 'existed before me' and reaches into virtual problems and questions where Aids in Western culture could become a collective crisis, which highlighted striated constructions of masculinity, thus constructions of sexuality in general and their very reality down to legislation and everyday life. Deleuze, rejecting the obvious labeling of sexualities, speaks subversively of "local and non-specific homosexuality" (Deleuze 2008b: 88) and that "the separated, partitioned sexes coexist in the same individual" (Deleuze 2008b: 51), a thoroughly alchemical position. This particular wound and its strands obviously is just one threshold in one specific project. However, it suggests that the dice-throw of uncomfortable feelings in practice might become pointers to the a-subjective qualities of something more than 'anything goes' (so often ascribed to Deleuze): by following their lines of flight, through and out of the frames of sentimentality, of the 'already-felt', the second hand experience.

Painting/drawing/editing with the image 'in-between' and the tension between *Becoming* and its re/presentation with different materialities, seems a way of approaching the 'complex act'—as decisions about the pragmatics of *living* differentiation in art practice. The attitude of "letting oneself act", be traversed by the virtual, as Villani puts it (Villani 2010, 77)—yet also traversed by temporally collaged, fugitive image-projections—this attitude is obviously one of focus and absorption; 'motivated', quoting here Michael Fried, "by the desire to escape the theatricalising consequences of the beholder's presence" (Fried 1980: 4) and at the same time to offer space for echoes of new becomings between visuals and beholders.

1. Grünewald's *Resurrection* accessible for example at http://www.wikipaintings.org; the manuscript of *Splendor Solis* at the British Library at http://www.bl.uk

References

BENJAMIN, W. (2002) *Selected Writings Vol. 3 1935–1938*, Cambridge, Mass. & London: The Belknap Press of Harvard University Press

DELEUZE, G. (2001) *Pure Immanence: Essays on a Life*, New York: Zone Books

—. (2004a) *Difference and Repetition*, London: Continuum

—. (2004b) *The Logic of Sense*, London: Continuum

—. (2008a) *Cinema 2. The Time Image*, London: Continuum

—. (2008b) *Proust and Signs: The Complete Text*, London: Continuum

FRIED, M. (1980) *Absorption and Theatricality: Painting and Beholder in the Age of Diderot*, Berkeley, London: University of California

HARLAND, B. (2009) *A Fragment of Time in the Pure State: Mapping Painting's Temporality through the Digital Image*, Saarbrücken: VDM Verlag Dr. Müller

LUCRETIUS. (1999) *On the Nature of the Universe*, Oxford: Oxford University Press

MOSÈS, S. (2009) *The Angel of History : Rosenzweig, Benjamin, Scholem*, Stanford, Calif.: Stanford General

VILLANI, A. (2010) 'The Insistence of the Virtual in Science and the History of Philosophy', in: Gaffney, P. ed. *The Force of the Virtual*, Minneapolis: University of Minnesota Press

VON BRASCH, M. (2012) *'Distance, However Near It May Be': Revisiting 'Aura' on the Axis between Painting and Digital Technology within a Deleuzian Framework of 'Becoming'*, University of Southampton. http://eprints.soton.ac.uk/346350

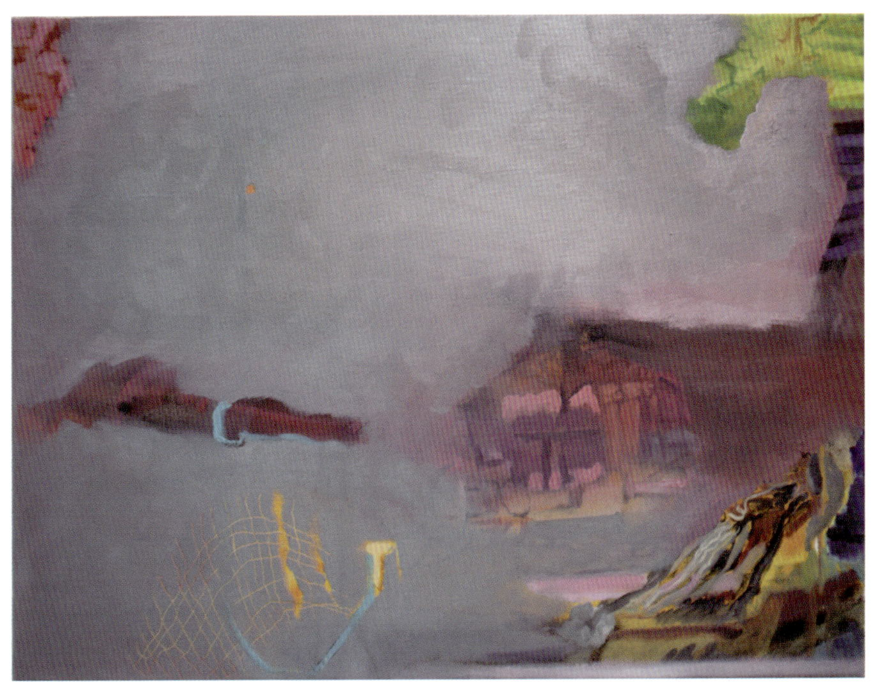

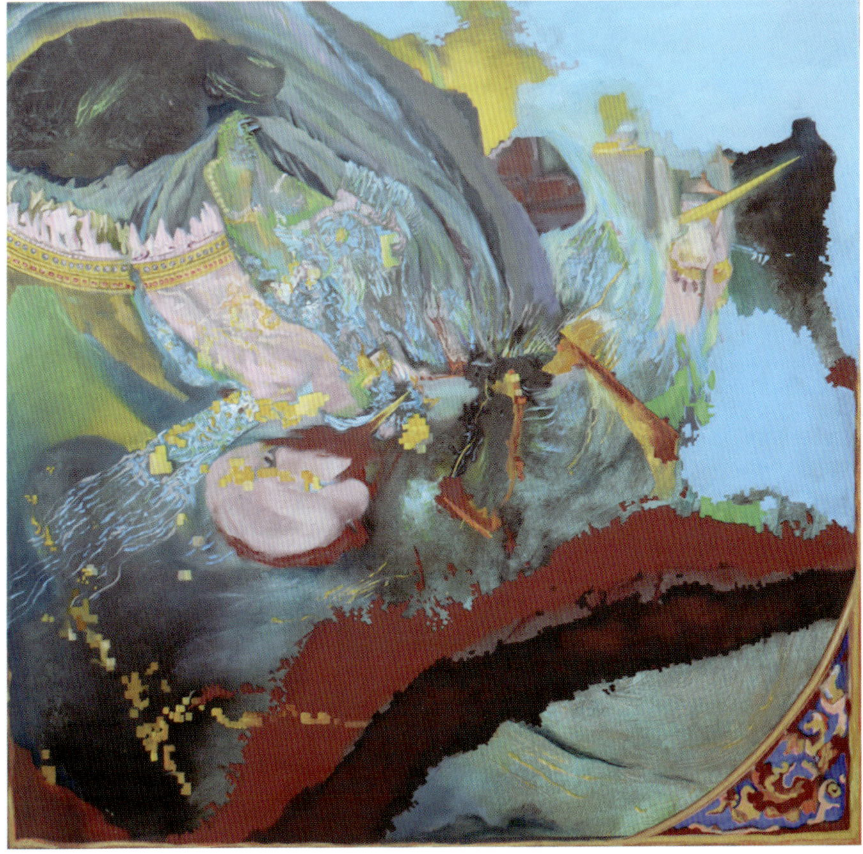

ABOVE:
Greyzone 1
(from *Empedocles
Assemblage*), oil on
canvas, 36 x 46cm

BELOW:
*Preceding/Forgotten
Spaces 1*, oil on
linen, 92 x 92cm

BETH HARLAND

Cut Scatter series

The *Cut Scatter* series of paintings is one of several in which I investigate picture-making through the fragmentation and re-inscription of existing images, invoking different temporalities simultaneously. The series reflects research of key pictorial moments in modernism, in particular Manet's paintings, but also such revolutionary works as Malevich's *0.10* exhibition, El Lissitsky's *Untitled (Rosa Luxemburg)* and the picture which historian T. J. Clark sees as the first Modernist painting: David's *Death of Marat*, painted at the end of the 18th Century. In his book *Farewell to an Idea*, Clark describes the time of modernism as one in which "contingency enters the process of picture making. It invades it." (Clark, 2001: 18)

A clear indication of a break with tradition in picture-making at this time can be seen in the movement away from *wholeness*, from 'coherence' of form and narrative; a challenge to the immediately comprehensible. One of the great criticisms of Manet in his day was that his paintings were 'unfinished', that they lacked coherence, there were different approaches in different areas of the painting, something that was deeply disturbing to many of his spectators. Manet's tendency towards the disintegration of classical unity of the picture seems paradoxical; he somehow gave a *salon*-style unity to an assemblage of heteronomous fragments.

I started the *Cut Scatter* series by collecting, and making, a set of source images which reflected such moments of pictorial reinvention, and experimented with methods of working with them to echo themes of contingency, chance and fragmentation. I made collages and drawings, and arrived at a system of composition that involved cutting up the printed source images (keeping them face down to avoid conscious compositional choices) into pieces that varied in size from a substantial percentage of the image to a tiny shard of it. I then dropped the fragmented images from up high, onto a grey studio floor, and photographed and painted the resulting chance-driven compositions. The uneven texture of the floor became the flecks indicating either depth or surface within each painting's ground.

The image sources for the series might best be grouped under the thematic 'ideals', suggesting idealization in artworks, in media representations, and in more personal evocations of place. To the images of modernist artworks mentioned above, I added: Manet's *Déjeuner sur L'Herbe* and *The Balcony*; film stills (choosing films that introduced a radical type of address to the viewer) from Antonioni's *La Notte*, *L'eclisse* and *Zabriski Point*, and Lynch's *Inland Empire*; and idealized landscapes, both impersonal (magazine adverts with mountains and gushing streams) and personal (photographs of forests and plants and drawings of structures).

I hope to convey something about complexity/thought/time, materially experienced in the way that is very particular to painting. This includes evoking the contradictory qualities of motion and stillness. As individual elements within a series, the paintings evolve, reflecting changing thoughts about process and decision, and different ways of addressing the figure/ground relationship. They withhold narrative information and establish a kind of distance in their address to the spectator. They present painting as investigation, the play of flatness and depth, and engage with pictorial history through the quotation of modernity's fragments, its residue.

References

CLARK, T. J. (2002) *Farewell to an Idea*, New Haven & London: Yale University Press

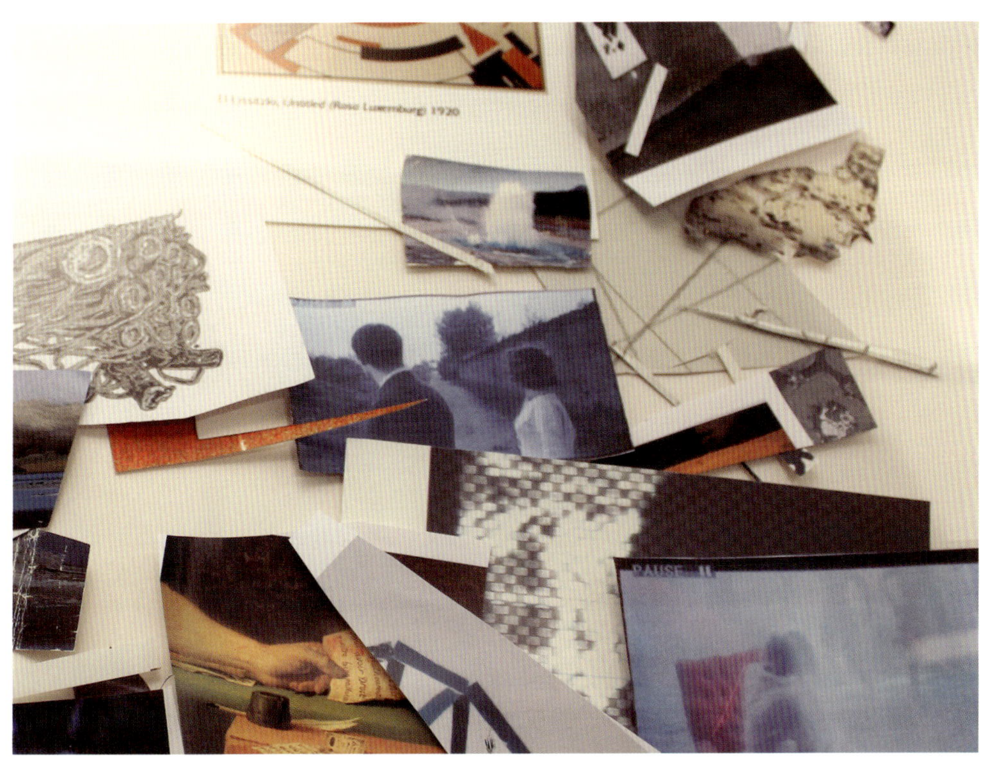
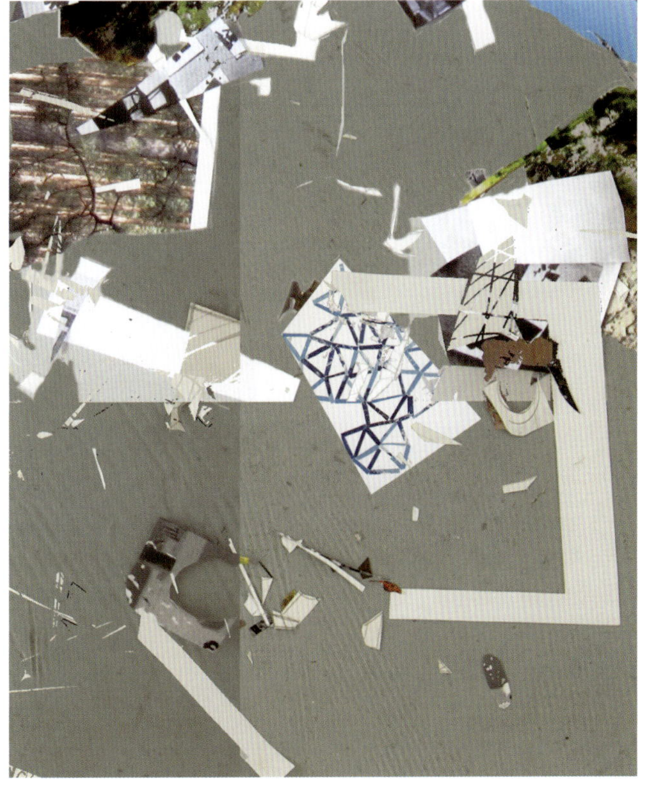

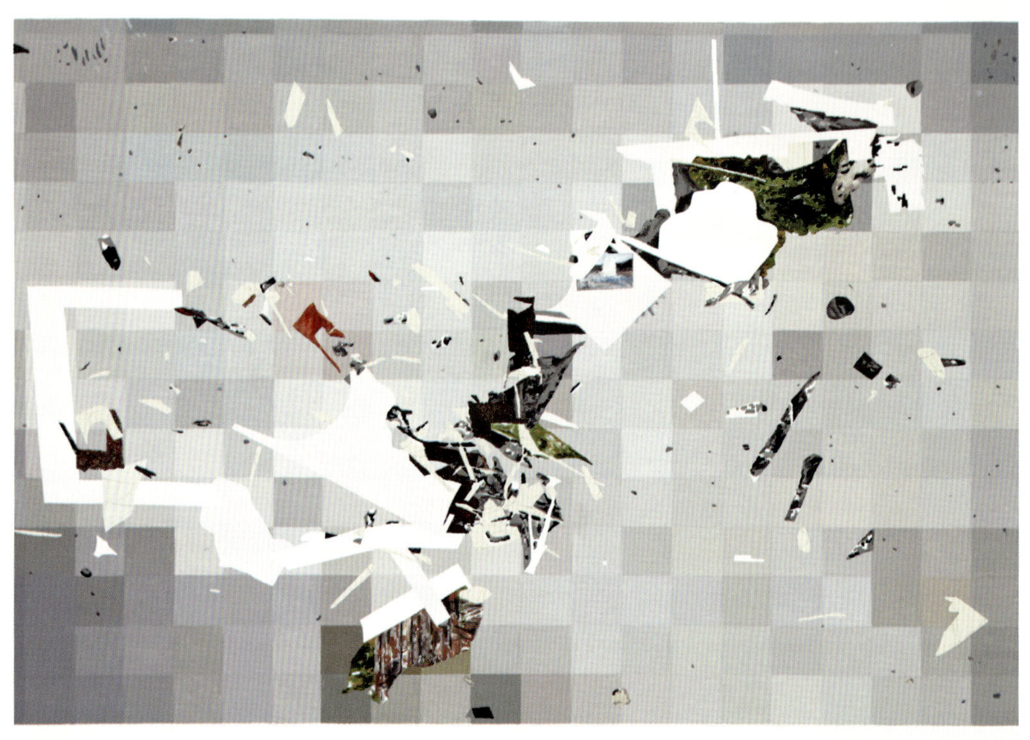

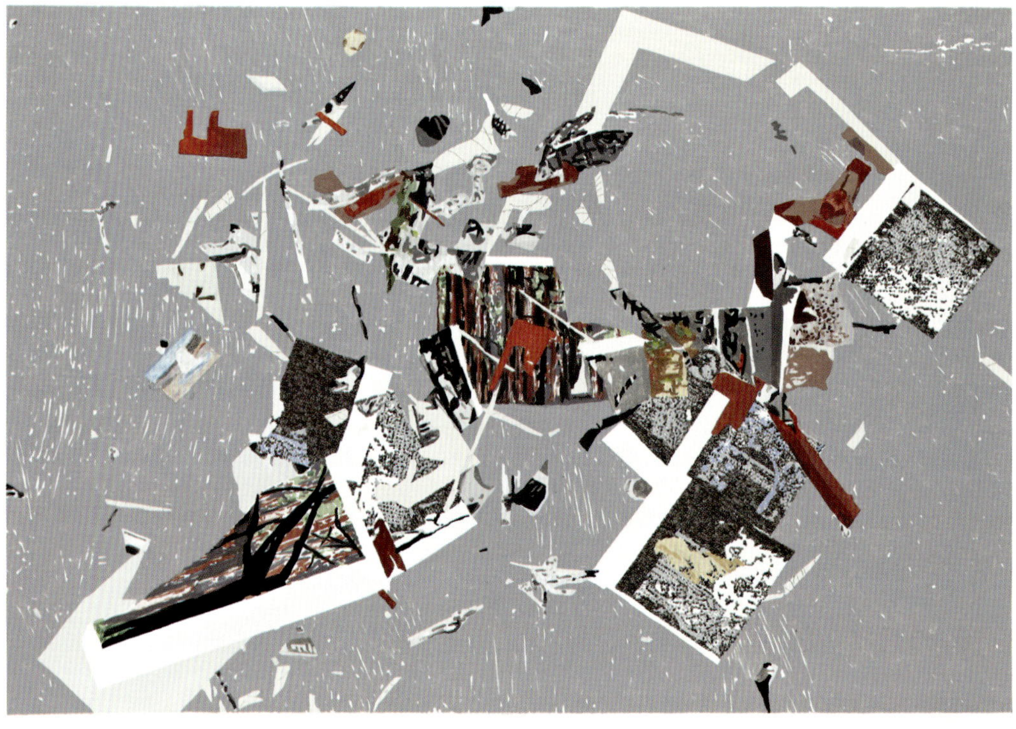

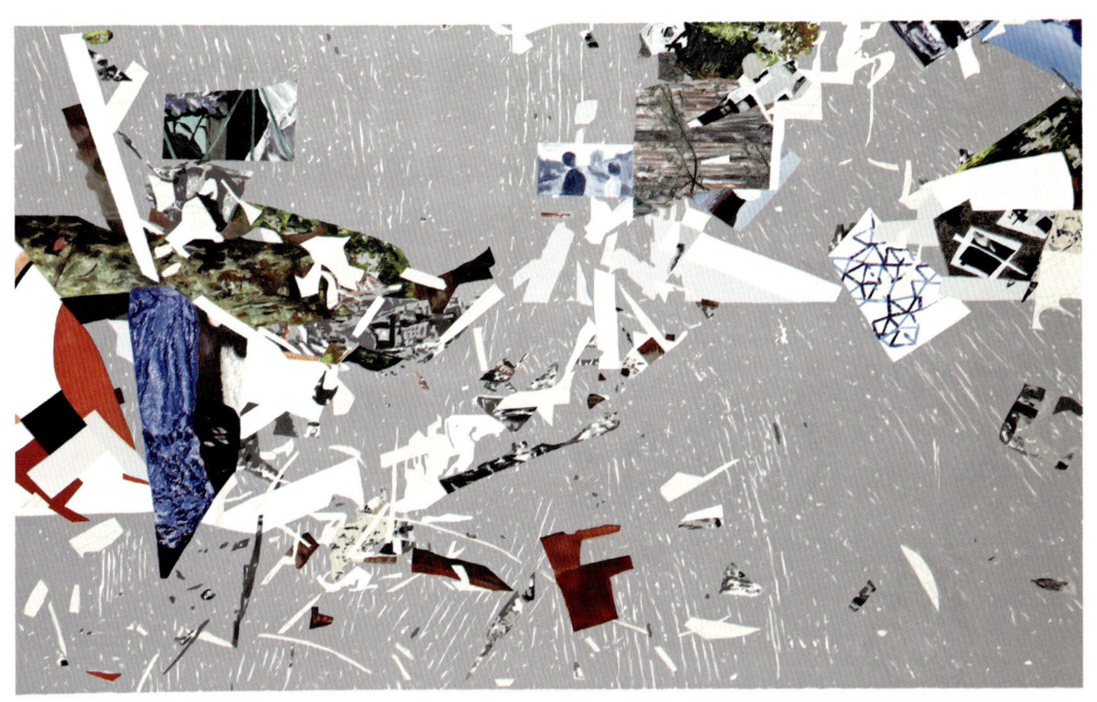

ABOVE: *Cut scatter 5*, oil on canvas, 111 x 167cm
OPPOSITE ABOVE: *Cut scatter 3*, oil on canvas, 91 x 121cm; OPPOSITE BELOW: *Cut scatter 1*, oil on canvas, 81 x 111cm

DONAL MOLONEY

'The Supplemental':
Transformations in painting processes

The transformation of source material is integral, rather than supplemental, to paintings I have made since 2010. My practice stems from an interest in how the activity of painting can be channelled and transformed through other media and processes from outside itself, such as sculpture, photography, weaving, video, and how this channelling can return back to painting. This stems from an interest in the ways in which paintings might operate as receptacles or containers of time.

The paintings I currently make are meticulously crafted and intricately detailed, taking between five and six months to complete. The use of detail, I think, gives a sense of gravity to the forms depicted. However, these forms perform, almost, as *wrong* signs, casting doubt on what one might be looking at. Most of the abstract shapes in these paintings have a figurative quality to them, and the figurative shapes look from different viewing distances like abstract marks, shapes and scribbles. Here, what oscillates is the viewing of the painting as a whole and how it breaks down into its constituent parts, pointing back to notions of the paintings production. This oscillation between figuration and abstraction is coupled with other oscillations; between flatness and depth, tension and release, and between material and the illusion of material. A shift occurs here between the "self contained repose" of the static painting and the dynamic activity of

viewing (Kandinsky, 1947: 57). Once the multitude of signs and planes of the painting coalesce into a form of suspense or tension, a sense of duration may be inferred between how the painting was constructed and the ways in which the viewer orchestrates their experience with the work. Ambiguity is used to cultivate curiosity in the viewer. Detail is there to initiate a response.

In my recent work I am still interested in non-representational formal concerns, such as seriality, but also in figuration. I am equally interested in subtly making evident the labour required to manipulate materials, so that the paintings might become a form of index of the time invested in their making. The result is that my paintings contain aspects of contemplative and meditative activity as well as a more physical playfulness with materials. How an image is painted is as important as what is painted; both work in tandem.

In his book *Looking at the Overlooked*, Norman Bryson makes an interesting observation about adding supplementary value to finished artefacts by re-presenting them. Bryson notes that Willem Kalf's painting *Still Life with Nautilus Cup* (1662) is subject to 'the paradox of the supplement' (Bryson, 1990: 126). By repeating a work of art through another work of art, the painted replica points to a state of *lack* in the original in how it continually needs *value* to be added to it (Bryson, 1990: 126). Bryson is persuasive in his argument that the painted copy "indicates a deficiency in the

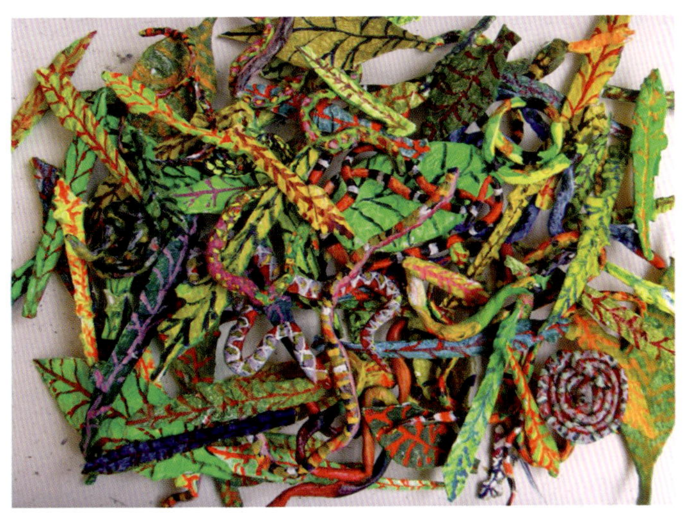

Macquette

original object" that will "not be remedied by the supplement, but contaminates it and so to speak hollows it out" (Bryson, 1990: 126). Because the copy, according to Bryson, usurps the original, the original 'loses its foundation' (Bryson, 1990: 126). However, this means that the painted copy also loses its foundation. Bryson calls this "disturbing" because it questions whether the objects that were painted were actually real in the first place or invented: "The ontological instability which Kalf's technique introduces has the effect of rendering substantiality uncertain, and this opens the doors of fantasy" (Bryson, 1990: 126).

In relation to my practice, Bryson's observation makes me question how I leave space in the source material I create so that I may begin to shift its meaning. My methods of collecting, creating and modifying source material aligns with Derek Pigrum and Andrew Stables' (2005: 2) *Four Registers of Transitional Practice*. Each register is a different method of transforming images and ideas. 'Diverse and paratactic' material in the form of drawings, photographs and notes are modified in order to connect divergent and complementary observations. This helps locate the limits of particular questions that will form more specific research (Pigrum, Stables, 2005: 3). The limitations of one method can be offset by highlighting the strengths of another, helping propose new applications for the different processes I use (Pigrum, Stables, 2005: 3).

According to Derek Pigrum (2005: 4), these Four Transitional Registers form the traits of Das Gegenwerk. The word 'Gegen' in German translates as both 'towards' and 'away' (Pigrum, Stables, 2005: 4). Thus, Pigrum states that Das Gegenwerk is the process of moving "towards the finished work, but also the work that is in opposition to the closure of the completed work". The registers of Das Gegenwerk provide cycles of 'provisionality and indeterminacy'; a filtering process where the original idea can be rethought and shaped through material processes on its way towards a painted image (Pigrum, Stables, 2005: 4).

I want to question whether, rather than being extraneous, these registers or processes that condition the content of my source material might also determine its wider cultural value. A key focus in my practice based research is the oscillation between the fiction represented by surface and the actual processes of the painting's construction. This investigation is underpinned by different perspectives on when processes becomes supplementary, or simplified to a means of achieving some end or result.

Rather than being a means to an end, the processes I use to generate imagery might be explicated through articulating the theoretical relationship between the symbolic information in the material and the performative forms of painting practice. This goes beyond the idea that the handmade aspect of contemporary painting is

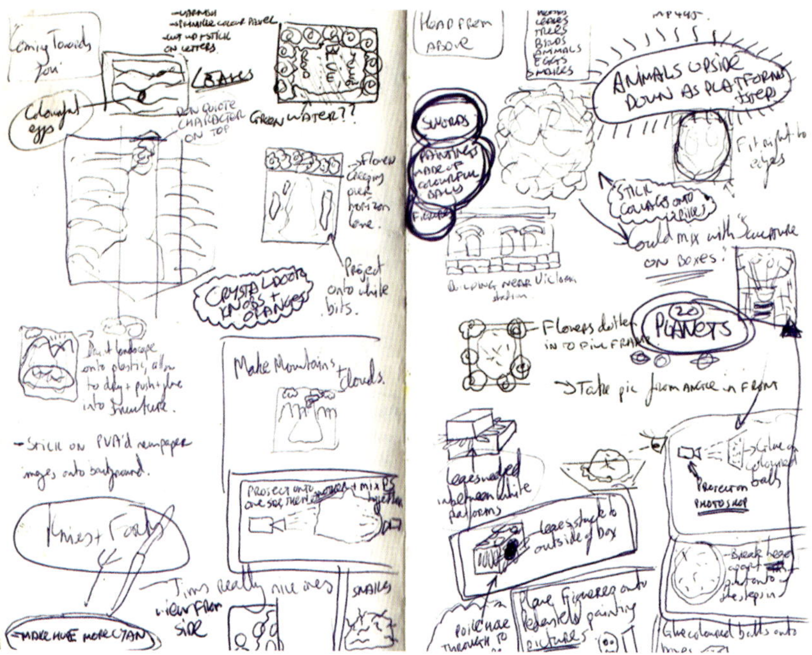

LEFT: Sketchbook

RIGHT: *Shrines*, acrylic on canvas, 42 x 52 cm, detail

solely a response or critique of the omnipresence of technology in everyday life. In fact, rather than ignoring technology many practices embrace it and employ it strategically with the handmade.

Kendall Walton (2008: 228) observed that the way in which a painting's surface is perceived is not 'veridical' or directly aligned with, the lengthy or quick processes of its making. Implied processes may act as another layer of illusion, playing out their symbiotic relationship with various pictorial illusions. Over the course of transforming source material artists continually re-evaluate their aims, allowing room for change in the process. I think these shifts or transitions in many artistic practices are inevitable. In relation to this, Irwin C. Leib (1991: 252) wrote: "We have a sense for the quality and fittingness of values, one kind with another, and this sense can be guiding for us, though we have always to make it more definite. Times change, values change". What Leib highlights is that artists must make way for these changes. This highlights questions about traces of processes used; questions about the relationship between medium, method and outcome as well as questions about the presence of the maker. The suggestion of how source material was transformed is integral, rather than supplemental, to how we look at a painting.

References

ADAMSON, G. (2007) *Thinking Through Craft*, Oxford: Berg Publishers

BRYSON, N. (1990) *Looking at the Overlooked, Four Essays on Still Life Painting*, London: Reaktion Books

KANDINSKY, W. (1979) *Point and Line to Plane*, New York: Dover Publications

LEIB, I. C. (1991) *Past, present and future: a philosophical essay about time*, Illinois: University of Illinois Press

PIGRUM, D. & STABLES, A. (2005) Qualitative Inquiry as Gegenwerk: Connections Between Art and Research. *International Journal of Qualitative Methods*, Vol. 4 (4), pp.1–15

WALTON, K. L. (2008) *Marvelous Images; on Values and the Arts*, Oxford: Oxford University Press

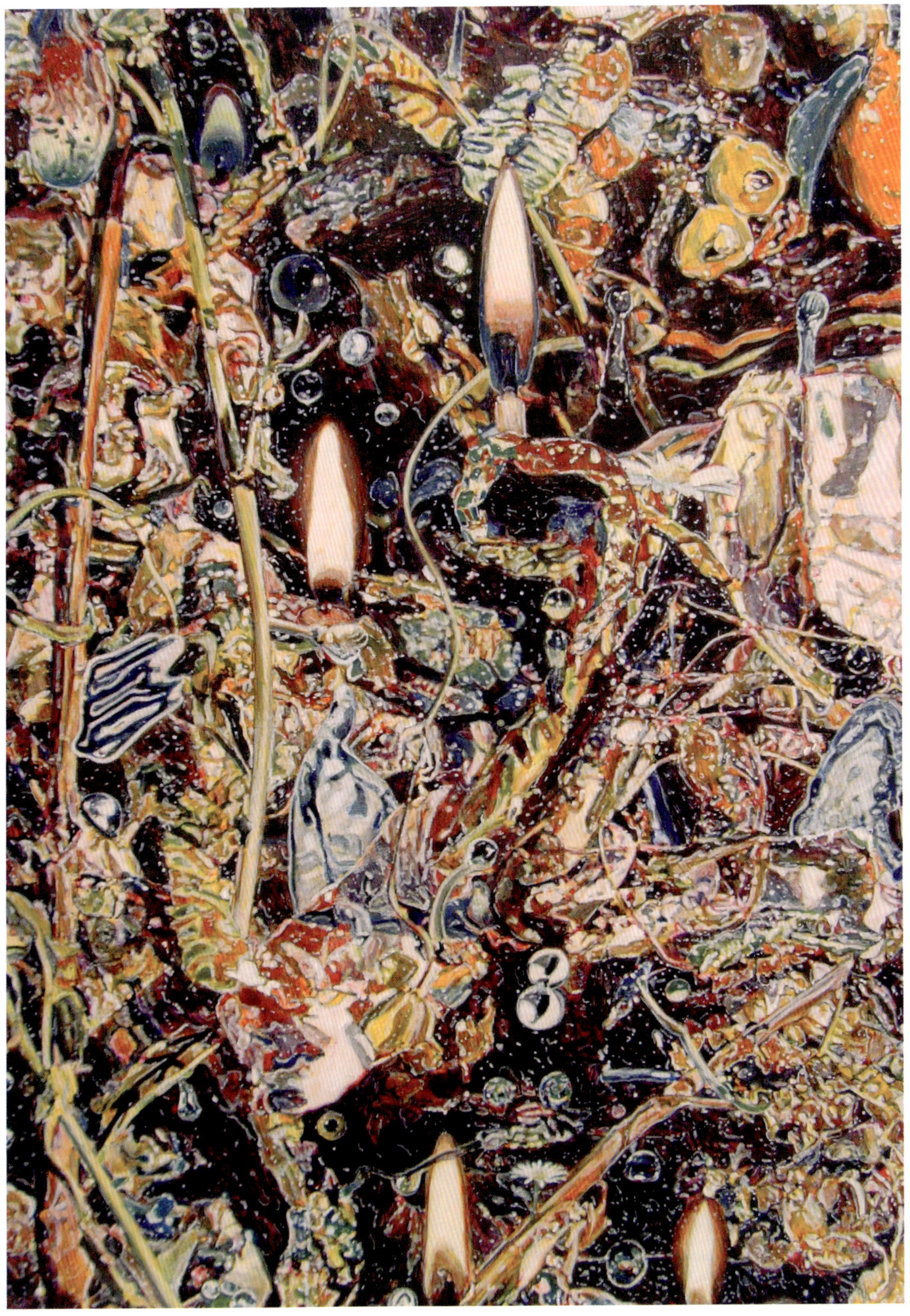

NINA PANCHEVA-KIRKOVA

Fragments of a Past: Socialist Realist Images in a Post-Communist Context

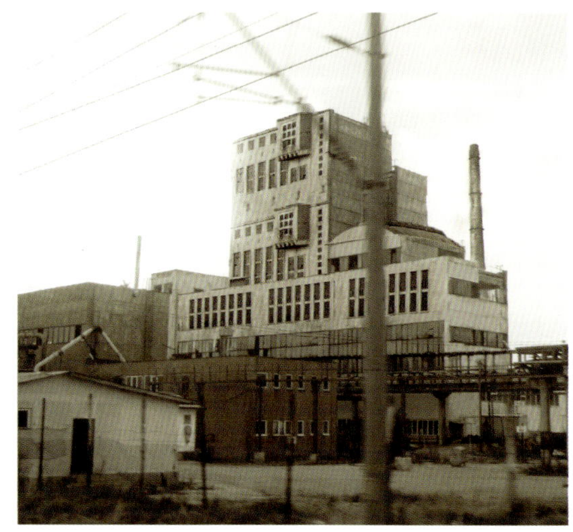

After the fall of the state communism, fine art in Bulgaria left the mediums of painting, graphics and sculpture in search of novel forms. At first sight the new, pluralistic subjects and mediums appear to reject the monologue of Socialist Realism and its claim to be the only one, authentic aesthetic. But how was it interpreted from a post-communist viewpoint? Nostalgia towards communism and aspiration for erasing the past have affected the debate to a great extent. Wreathed in a mist of narratives and memories, Socialist Realism has been recounted rather than examined.

In this context my work explores how (or if) the communist heritage in fine art has been over-come, and how discussions of this transition could be explored in a contemporary art practice. Old press photographs and images of Socialist Realist sculptures have been used as source material and through their decontextualization and fragmenta-tion, my practice seeks to explore continuity and discontinuity between the two periods.

As examples of this artistic procedure two series of my paintings will be discussed.

Series: Fragments of a Past

A photograph of a big factory, an old black and white photograph. Date and author are unknown. It appears to be one of the seemingly documentary photographs taken during

communism to 'display facts'. But not quite. David Hockney says that "the best use for photography… is photographing other pictures. It is the only time it can be true to its medium, in the sense that it's real" (Hockney, 1981: 8). So how true is the old photograph? The historical work is regarded by White as a "narrative prose discourse that purports to be a model, or icon of past structures and processes in the interest of explaining what they were by representing them" (White, 1973: 2). According to the communist ideology, economics is the base of any society consequently the represented industrial building could be an architectural embodiment of ideological success. The building appears to be self-sufficient; it resembles more of a monument than a factory. It does not tell a story about a successful industry irrespective of the author's intentions. The rigid composition, flat sky and detachment of the architectural structure bring Bernd and Hilla Becher's typologies to the viewer's mind. Having turned a factory into a memorial of ideological illusions of communism, this photograph has created an image that appears to be alternative to the dominant ideological one.

Foucault emphasises the fictive character of the historical reconstruction (Foucault, 2002). The series *Fragments of the Past* uses the old photograph as its starting point. Through an act of re-seeing the image and turning into painting it has been alienated from its claim to present

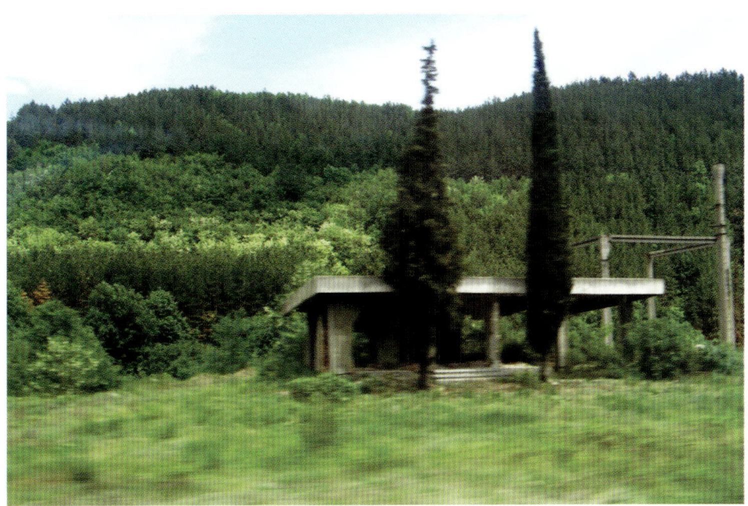

RIGHT: Ruins
OPPOSITE: Factory

a historical fact. Why is the image important then? The choice of the photograph itself makes it substantial and turns it into a key moment or space. The idea of seeing this as a documentary image defers to an attempt to discover structural oppositions in it, oppositions that explore the subject rather than describing it.

The paintings do not try to repeat or describe the photographs. "In front of a photograph, the feeling of 'denotation', or, if one prefers, of analogical plenitude, is so great that the description of a photograph is literally impossible" (Barthes, 1977: 18). Instead the pictures seek to explore the hidden structures that form the institutions, responsible for the arts in the country, as well as the network of power that seems to predetermine the changes after the collapse of communism. "It is not the artist's job to restore a 'supposed' reality that the search for knowledge, techniques and wealth never stops destroying, only to reconstruct a version thought for a while to be more credible, and which will have to be abandoned in its turn" (Lyotard, 1991: 128).

In the process of developing the series, every painting has led to discovery of new structural oppositions and thus to a new painting. The initial relation between a public space (the factory) and a private one (house) has become more complex by adding images of new spaces, both private and public. Fragments of the communist party's quarter, the national bank, monuments and key communist buildings and public spaces have expanded the search for new oppositions that could explore relations between fine art and the art institutions. Positioning the canvases in a grid has been incorporated in the series, so adding a new sequential experience and avoiding once again the concept of linearity.

The Island of Utopia

Two elements—a desolated building and a cypress, connected and juxtaposed through a photograph, have become the initial point of the painting. The photograph was taken around an abandoned factory in Bulgaria and almost accidently brought together a part of the neglected structure and two cypresses. Their relations evoked Arnold Bocklin's painting *The Isle of the Dead* to my mind. The mysterious, almost surreal atmosphere in the painting without a particular time frame has reminded me of the concept of communism as mythology, an idea supported by the aims of the communist ideology to re-build society and re-invent man.

Thomas More describes an island in his vision of a utopian society. In Bulgaria communism created an island, a closed society alienated from the outside world. In my painting *The Island of Utopia,* the rocky shore from the Bocklin's work is replaced by a concrete one, and the rocks by buildings. There are no doors or windows on the

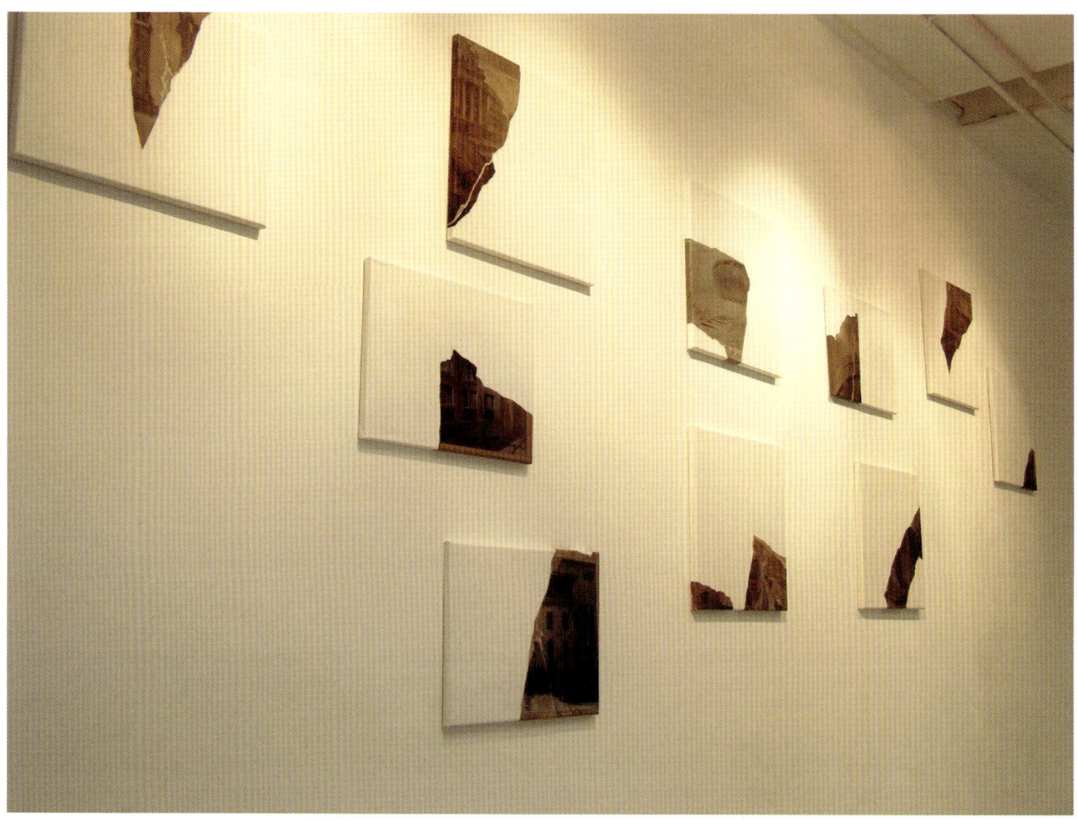

constructions and their function remains unclear, they could be either city or pagan sanctuary, or maybe monuments. The place looks quiet and austere, it might be forgotten or neglected. Or just not frequently visited. According to Marx "socialism was to be developed from its Utopian stage to its scientific stage" (Popper, 1945: 79). The painting *The Island of the Utopia* represents a stage of an 'accomplished utopia', a period after the communist regime took place. It pictures myth built as an artificial construction. The relations between layers of meanings hidden within the image of the abandoned factory and Bocklin's work have been explored through the process of developing the painting. The images have been destructed, their elements re-seen and re-built in the painting. It juxtaposes in a new way these components and seeks to explore communism in its ambivalence—as a mythology and rational construction; as praised and detested; as forgotten, but still extant.

References

BARTHES, R. (1977) *Image–Music–Text*, London: Fontana Press

BOIA, L. (1998) *Myths in Romanian Communism*, Bucharest: Nemira

FOUCAULT, M. (2002) *The Archaeology of Knowledge*, London: Routledge

HOCKNEY, D. (1981) *The Artist's eye: Looking at Pictures in a Book at the National Gallery, 1 July–31 August, 1981.* London: The National Gallery

LYOTARD, J.-F. (1991) *The Inhuman. Reflections on Time*, Cambridge: Polity Press

MARX, K. & ENGELS, F. (1976) *On Literature and Art*, Moscow: Progress Publishers

MIHAYLOVA, V. (2011) The Case Bulgaria. Contemporary Art beyond the Battlefield of Language Games towards Strategies of Possible Political Decisions, in *Nail magazine*, issue 4, 8.11.2011

POPPER, K. (1945) *The Open Society and Its Enemies*, Volume 2, London: Routledge

WHITE, H. (1973) *Metahistory*, Baltimore & London: The John Hopkins University Press

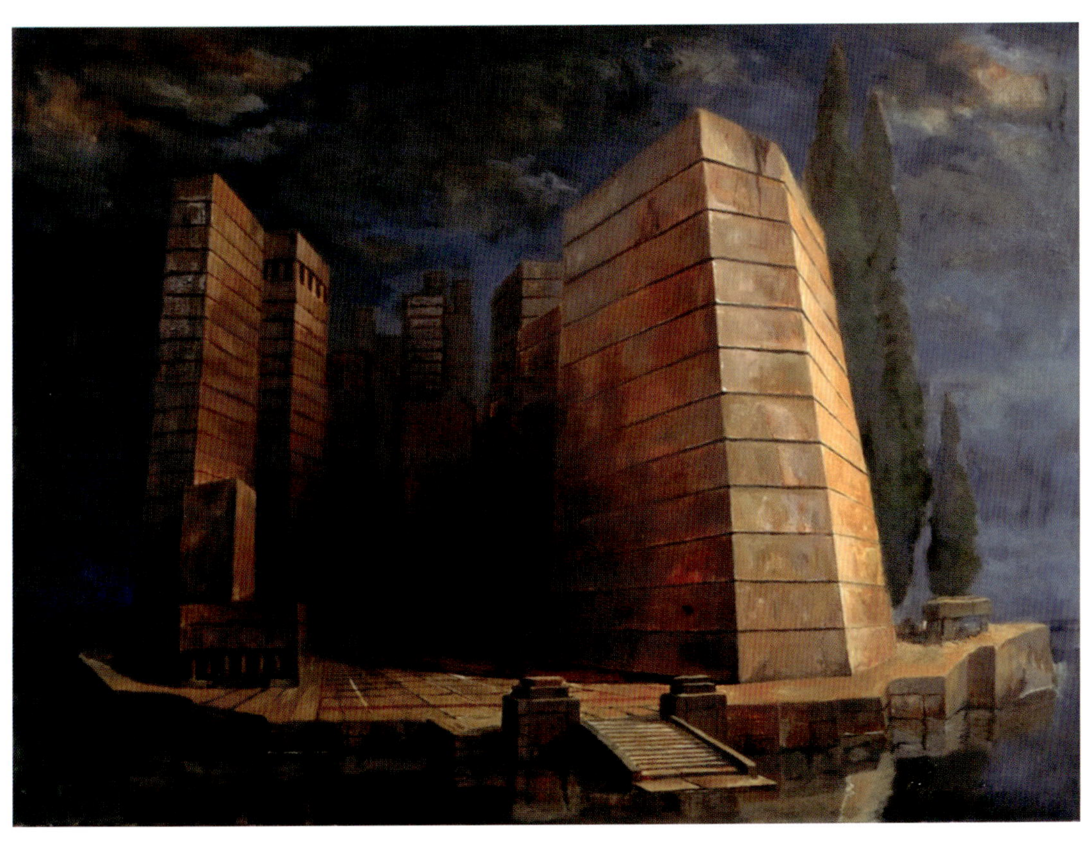

ABOVE: *The Island of the Utopia*, oil on canvas, 80 x 115 cm
OPPOSITE: *Fragments of a Past*, 100 x 220 cm (installation size)

Lindsey Adams is an artist based in Derbyshire.

Paul Goodfellow is a PhD candidate at
Northumbria University, Newcastle-upon-Tyne.

Johanna Love is Senior Lecturer in Fine Art/
Photography at University of Northampton and
Associate Lecturer at the Universities of Brighton,
Anglia Ruskin and University of the Arts London.

Rachel Sharp is a PhD candidate at Northumbria
University, Newcastle-upon-Tyne.

constructive imagination | image and composition | picture/ tableau | complex acts | transformation | modified | bricolage | hinge | re-seeing | emerging double | latent content | extraction | construction | permutations | plasticity | model | interwoven | materiality | aura | entropy | performative | tenor | cognition | subjectivities | absorbing | fragmentation | oscillate | layers | topology | gist | mediation | echo | de-composition | sideways | distraction | temporality | performative | supplemental | quotation | metanarrative | resonance | symbiotic | technology | image search | interactive | capture | system | simulating | strategies | looking away | supplement | becoming | destruction | fragment | superformula | reference | re-inscription | chance | marking | shadow | hybridise | dissociation | decipher | re-reading

Rebecca Fortnum | Kate Hawkins | Marc Hulson | Jim Threapleton

Marius Von Brasch | Beth Harland | Donal Moloney | Nina Pancheva-Kirkova

Lindsey Adams | Paul Goodfellow | Johanna Love | Rachel Sharp

LINDSEY ADAMS

Colletto Series

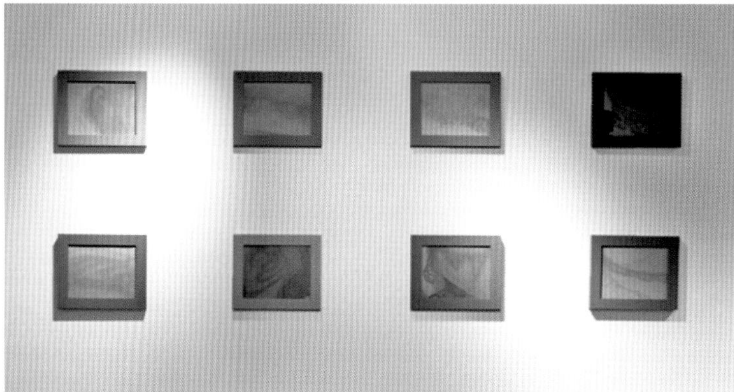

These works, the *Colletto* series, demonstrate my ongoing fascination with the way forms can be changed by differing light sources, both as reflection and shadow. They relate contextually to water colour and oil paintings from the 1970s and 80s, that were made as preparatory sketches for larger paintings, which concern themselves with looking at the atmospheric qualities of light passing through diaphanous fabric, a subject that I have returned to again and again. In these early paintings I often found myself more absorbed in the painting of those abstract parts than in the rest of the image represented, and it is this that I explore in the current series of works.

For these paintings using vintage collars that my mother wore, I found that I needed to take photographs to achieve the desired quality of (low) light and shadow. I also needed to take shots in physical positions that it would have been impossible to use if painting from the subject matter directly. I then worked with the photographs as I would have worked from 'life', that is to say, allowing my own aesthetic judgement to determine how true to life, or not, the final painting would be.

Lighting sources that modify or transform objects open up a world in which the imaginary can become a key player and perception is challenged.

I am interested in the way we are conditioned to see, and want to make paintings that demand different ways of looking. Several works within this current series of paintings have an ambivalence relating to the spatial depth and an ambiguous focus within the cast shadows to which the eye is drawn. These appear to hover in an indeterminate space, despite being fixed and shallow.

Somewhere in this uncertainty, the viewer's gaze is held and the painting can gently speak…

ABOVE: Installation
OPPOSITE: Contact Sheet
p.50 ABOVE: *Colletto 7*, 2012; BELOW: *Colletto 5*, 2011
p.51 ABOVE: *Colletto 8*, 2012; BELOW: *Colletto 9*, 2012
Oil on canvas, each 25 x 20cm unframed

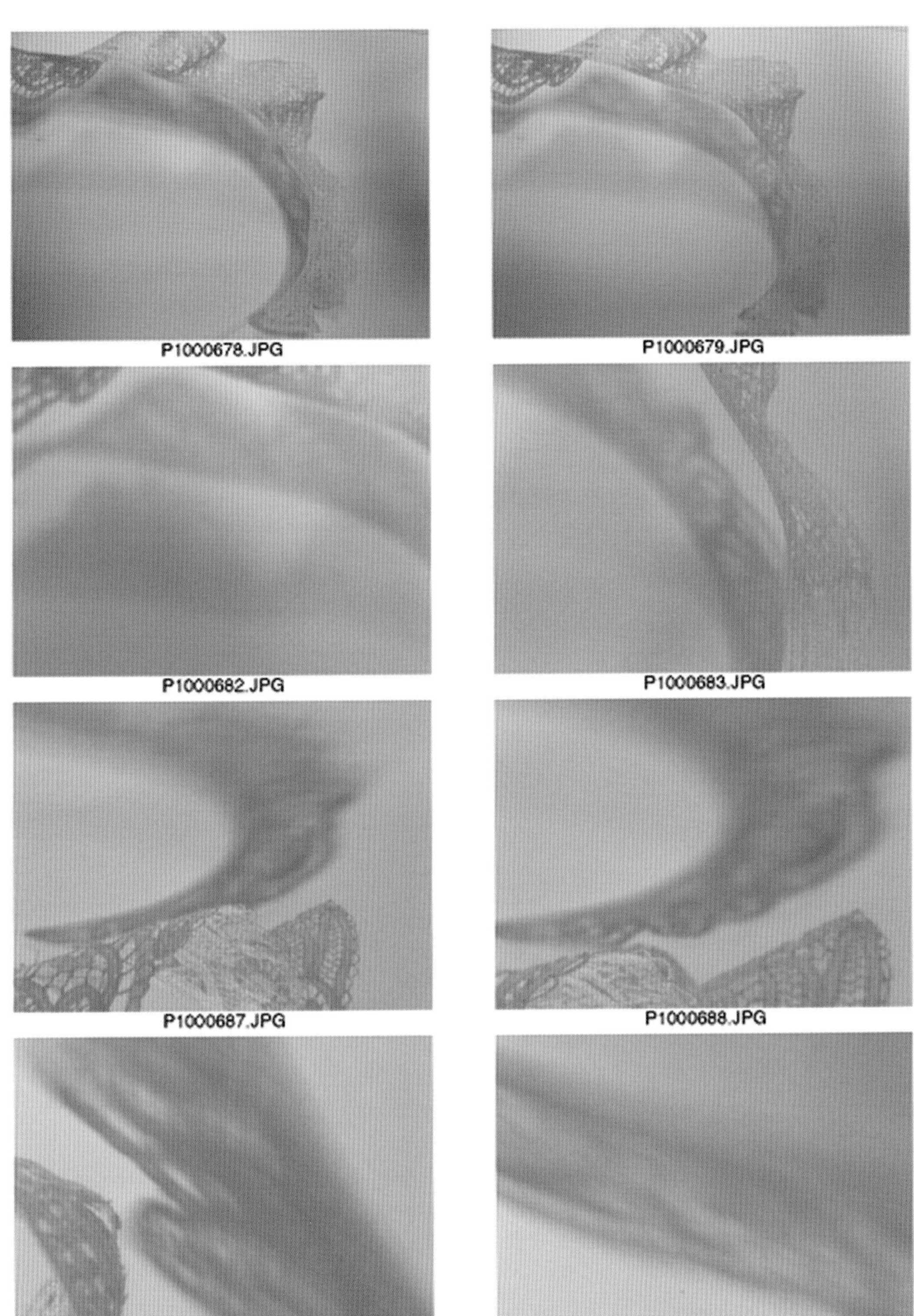

P1000678.JPG

P1000679.JPG

P1000682.JPG

P1000683.JPG

P1000687.JPG

P1000688.JPG

P1000692.JPG

P1000693.JPG

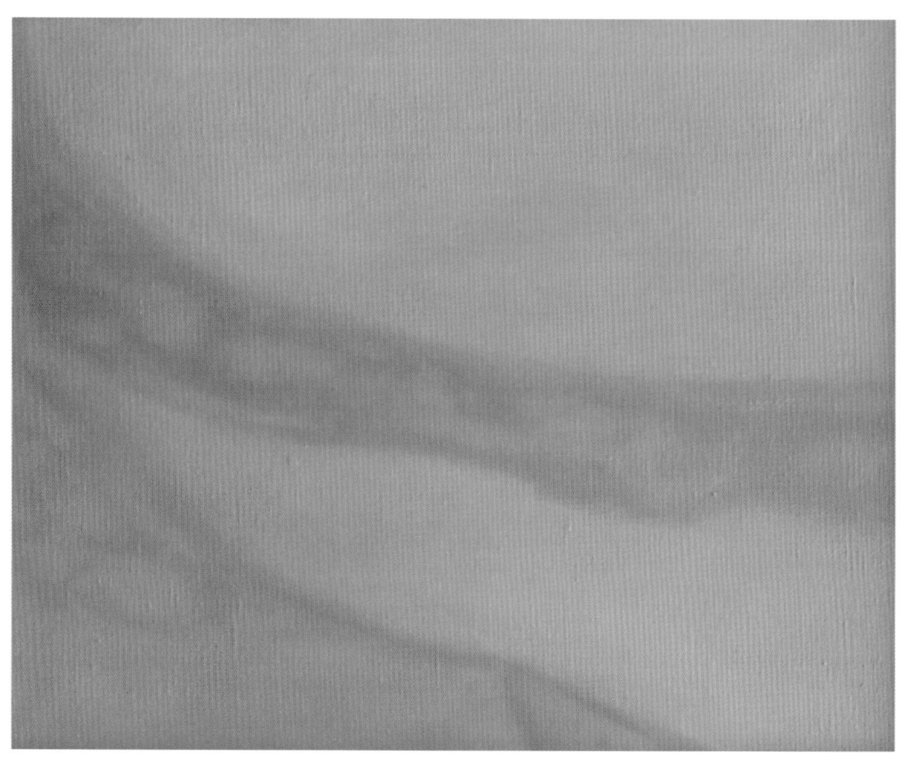

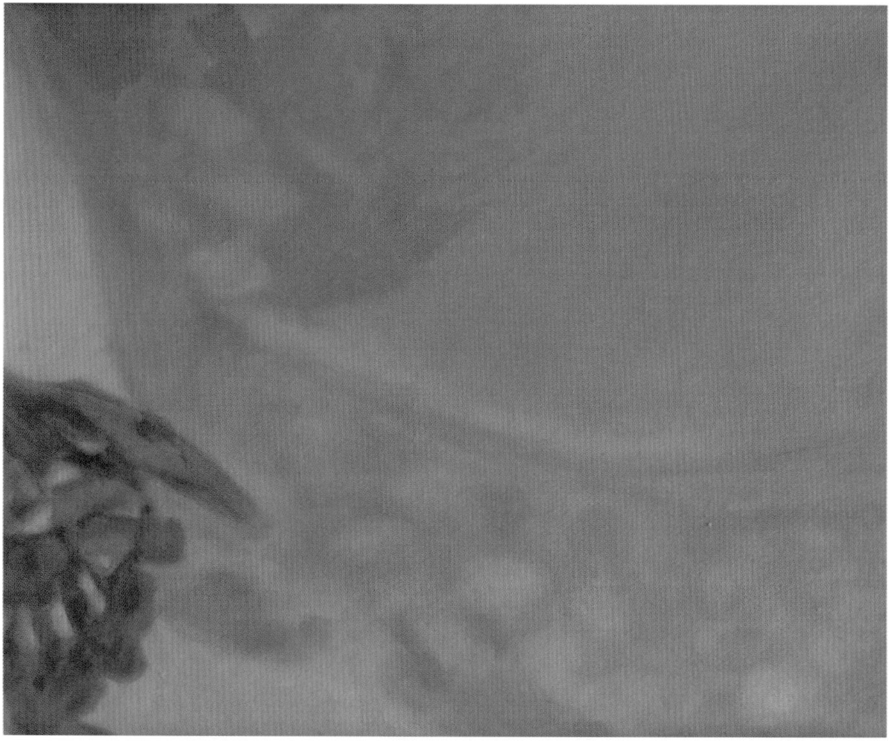

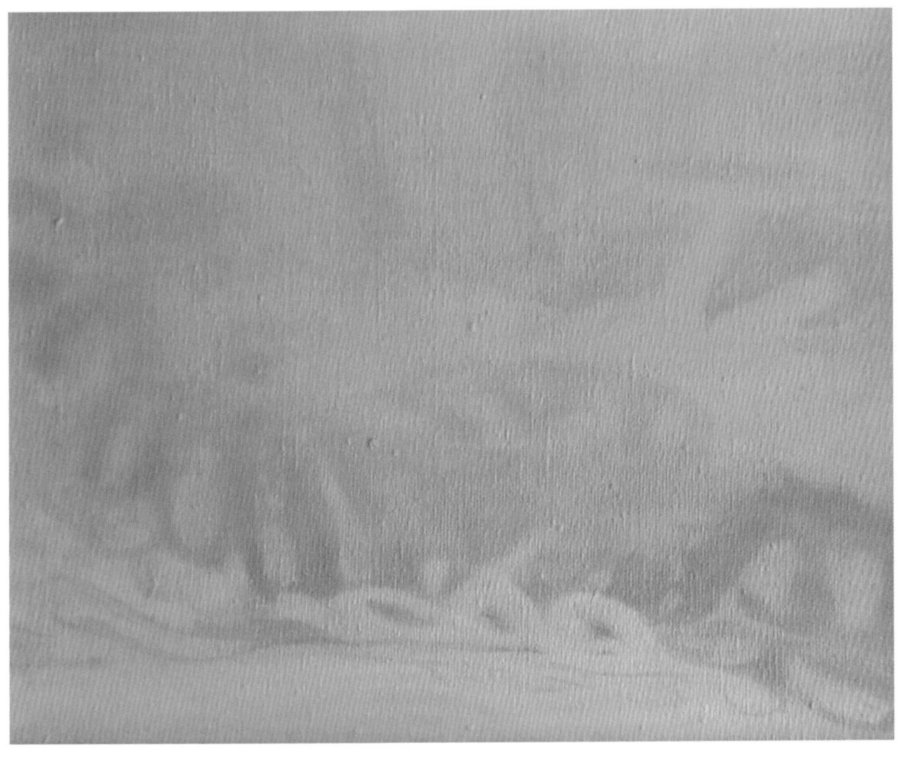

PAUL GOODFELLOW

Sampling of photographs and the 'Spectrum of Authorship'

This paper discusses the artist's process and suggests a taxonomic system for art objects, the *Spectrum of Authorship*, which positions work along a spectrum of authorship from machine or system made, to man-made art. Taking a systems art perspective the paper reflects upon the ideas of Chevrier (2012), on the distinctions between an image and picture, and how this can be reflected along a spectrum of authorship. Chevrier noted several criteria that distinguish a picture from an image. Firstly a picture is an autonomous object, whereas the image is reproducible. Secondly, in compositional terms the image can be delivered fully composed, effectively circumnavigating the conscious construction process required of the picture. Thirdly in terms of reception, the picture is confrontational in the sense that the construction process is specifically aimed at the viewer. Finally whilst an image may allow us to see something, a picture has contained within it an experience of something. With these distinctions in mind this paper contends that all plane based visual work can sit along a spectrum from image to picture, a *Spectrum of Authorship*. To illustrate this idea the artist's work is now described and classified in relation to the *Spectrum of Authorship* between system made images and man-made pictures.

Systems Art developed in the late 1960s as a branch of conceptual art that considered the emergent ideas of system science. This work often dealt with the underlying rules of production and reception of the art object. The systems artist Jack Burnham predicted a process of de-objectification within art. He proposed that the cultural obsession with the art object, was being overtaken by an understanding of systems and the relationships between art objects. Burnham noted "These new systems prompt us not to look at the skin of objects, but at those meaningful relations within and between their visible boundaries." (Burnham, 1968: 369–70). My work is, in part, a mediation on the use of systems in the production of art objects and questions the autonomy of objects produced through such systems.

System walks

The artist applies a systems approach to the production of the art objects and to the subject material of environment, to produce art from conceptually motivated walks named *System walks*. Walking is a direct way of experiencing a place qualitatively, and a useful way of capturing data quantitatively through photographic images. There is though a tension between the technology of image capture and the aesthetic perceptions of experiencing a place. This duality

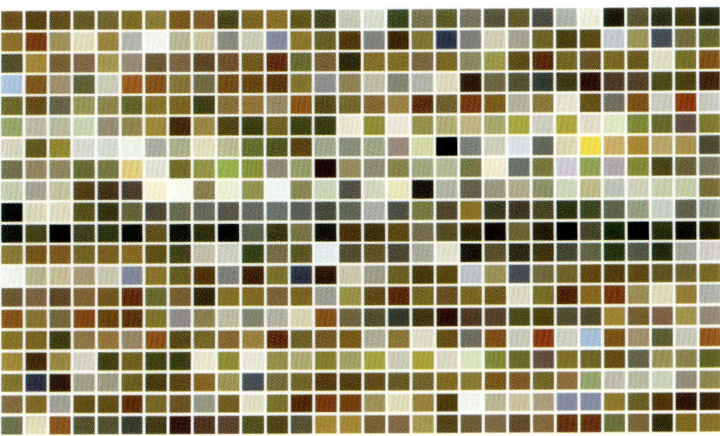

of the objective and subjective is accommodated in the ideas of Psychogeography, as described by Guy Debord, in *Theory of the Dérive* (Debord, 1997). The walks made are a private performance that is recorded. The work made from the walks is a culmination of organizing and abstracting the recorded information in a systematic way to produce *images*, and then transcending this order to construct *pictures*.

During a walk the artist carries a GPS unit to log key information, such as path coordinates and altitude, and a time-lapse camera worn on the chest, to passively capture photographs at fixed time intervals. This removes the 'authorial intent' from the process, as the artist cannot make compositional and framing decisions. At this stage the camera is merely sampling the colour values, whilst independently the artist experiences the walk, unencumbered by the need to manage or curate the experience.

In the studio the sequences of photographs are turned into stop-motion films and are used as the basis to produce all subsequent art objects. The first type of work is created by sampling a single colour value from each frame. These colour values can be selected either randomly using a computer program, or interactively using a digital drawing tablet and pen. In this work, the sampled colours are laid out as a grid of pixels, or squares of colour, starting in the upper left hand corner of the screen working down the screen from left to right. The process can be repeated indefinitely and each iteration of the work derives a different range and composition of colours.

In the second example, the same process of real-time colour sampling takes place, but this time the colours are represented as spots. The sampled spots are scaled and superimposed onto the original images. This adds a compositional, and an additional aesthetic element to the work. There is still a strong dialectical relationship with technology in this work. Walter Benjamin in *The Work of Art in the Age of Mechanical Reproduction* (Benjamin, 2008) noted that whilst technology has long been a part of human society modern technology transforms the spatio-temporal co-ordinates of experience. He used the Lithograph to illustrate this point noting that whilst it is capable of producing many copies of a work each will be unique to the time and place it was produced due to the inherent variability in the process. Likewise the systems employed here to produce these works in real-time captures a unique work that, whilst based on the original source material, is a specific response to the material and the gestures employed at the time of interaction.

In the final, more visually complex work, colours are extracted from the photographs, but

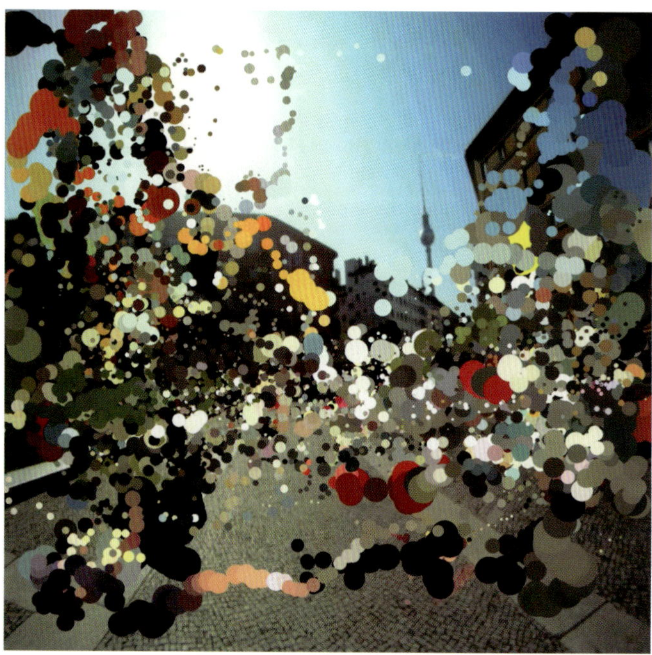

this time the shape that represents the samples are drawn and painted by hand. The system has suggested visual solutions on shape, colour and composition, but the final work is a summation of the experience of the walks and the experience of working with the system. Paint is layered and elements appear and disappear during the painting process as painting decisions override the algorithmic system decisions at the technology stage. Each painting produced is unique, non-repeatable, and acts as the end of a particular branch of the system.

Thus the art system produced for any given *System Walk* is composed of the walk, the iterative art objects and the paintings. The paintings acting as an end game for the system or that branch of the system as the painting contains decisions that cannot be fully understood or accommodated by the system. Thus it can be suggested that images are reproducible and repeatable products of a system, but pictures transcend the system from which they where built and cannot be identically reproduced due to the complexity of the construction process in paint.

Thus if we consider the *Spectrum of Authorship* diagrammatically the art objects described here can be laid along the spectrum from image to picture. All of the art objects are products of the system, with photographic images being system inputs, and pictures being system outputs. Thus at one end of the system are images, the passively captured photographs created without direct authorship. Moving further along the spectrum information from the photographs is abstracted into colour field works. These images contain no compositional decisions, other than laying out the samples on a sequential grid system. Moving closer to a picture are the spot images that can contain both colour field and compositional decisions. Finally the paintings are pictures, as they are produced through the experience of the walk and the rules of the system and the internal experience of both. They are physically constructed and this is inherent in the final work.

References

CHEVRIER, J. F. (2012) Seminar at Central Saint Martin's College of Art, London

BURNHAM, J. (1968) *Beyond Modern Sculpture*, London: Allen Lane

DEBORD, G. (1997) *Theory of the Derive*, Atlantic Books

BENJAMIN, W. (2008) *The Work of Art in the Age of Mechanical Reproduction*, London: Penguin

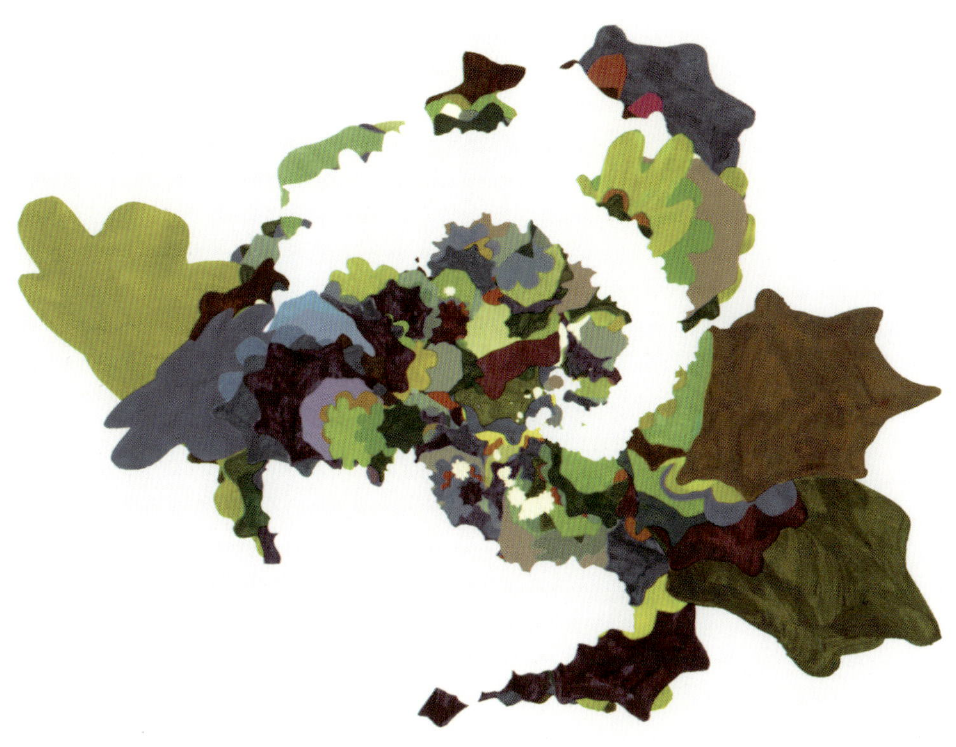

System Walk: Airigh-Drishaig 2011–ongoing
Pencil, ink and gouache on paper 42 x 59.4cm

JOHANNA LOVE

My current practice explores how digital photo-graphic landscape images and drawings of dust may sit together within the same pictorial surface to open up new possibilities of reading space and bringing about new apprehensions of temporality and mortality.

The artworks are constructed in two stages, firstly the digital photographic printed image. I am interested in how a photographic image might sit at the verge of recognition and provide an *almost* blank 'field' of vision, particularly through natural phenomena such as fog, which dissolves and distances the reading of the space.

The second stage to the work is the drawing of dust directly onto the photographic printed surface. Dust and debris is captured on small glass sheets, which have been left out for up to a month on the studio floor. These glass sheets are then scanned into the computer to create digital images. The drawings are made by placing the photographic printed image flat onto a drawing board. Using a graphite pencil, the marks are then drawn directly onto the print surface. The drawing emerges slowly, copied from small printed images of scanned dust and debris.

Each particle of dust is made as a visible marking. One of my intentions for the drawing of dust on the prints is to draw attention to the concealment of the materiality of the image made through digital photographic technologies. The digital image is separate from the inevitable decay of the material world. Drawing on and physically marking the surface of the photographic print is a strategy I use to reassert the presence of my own hand, my mark as author, into the digital process, generating an immediate indexical link to my own presence.

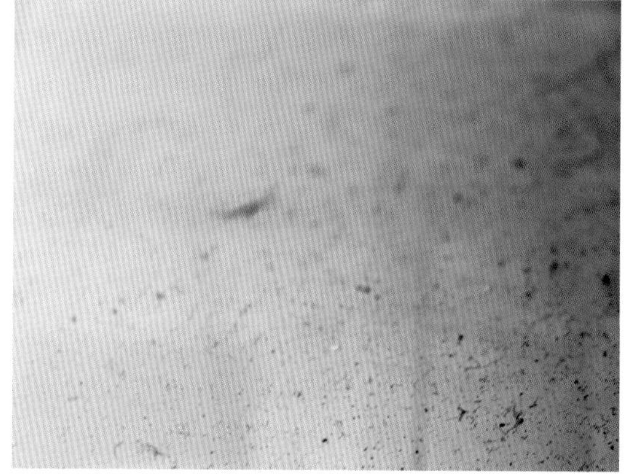

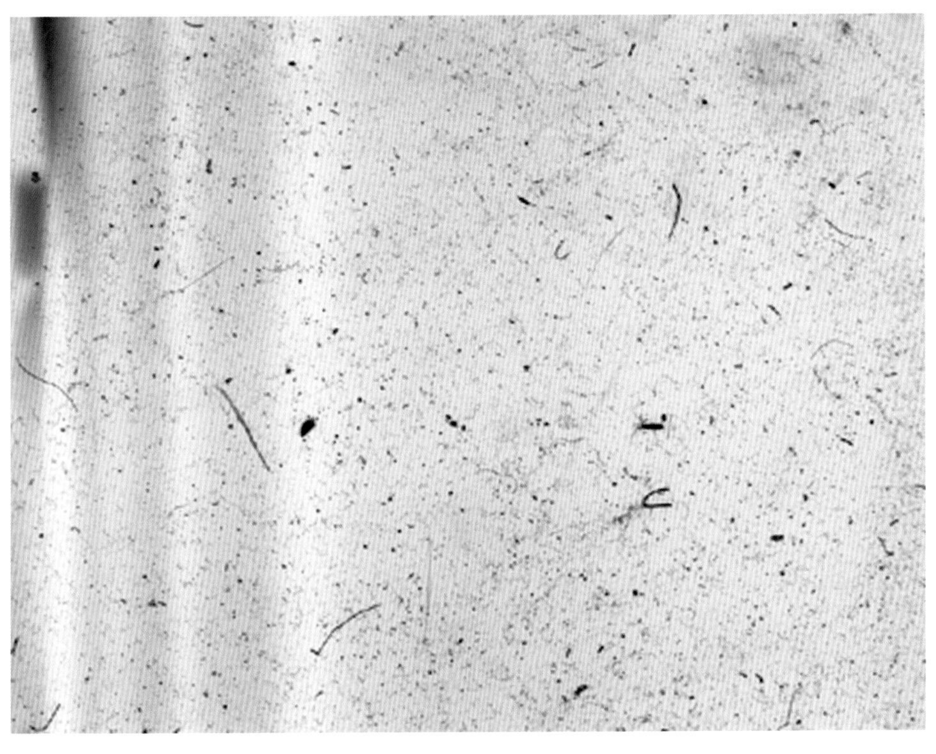

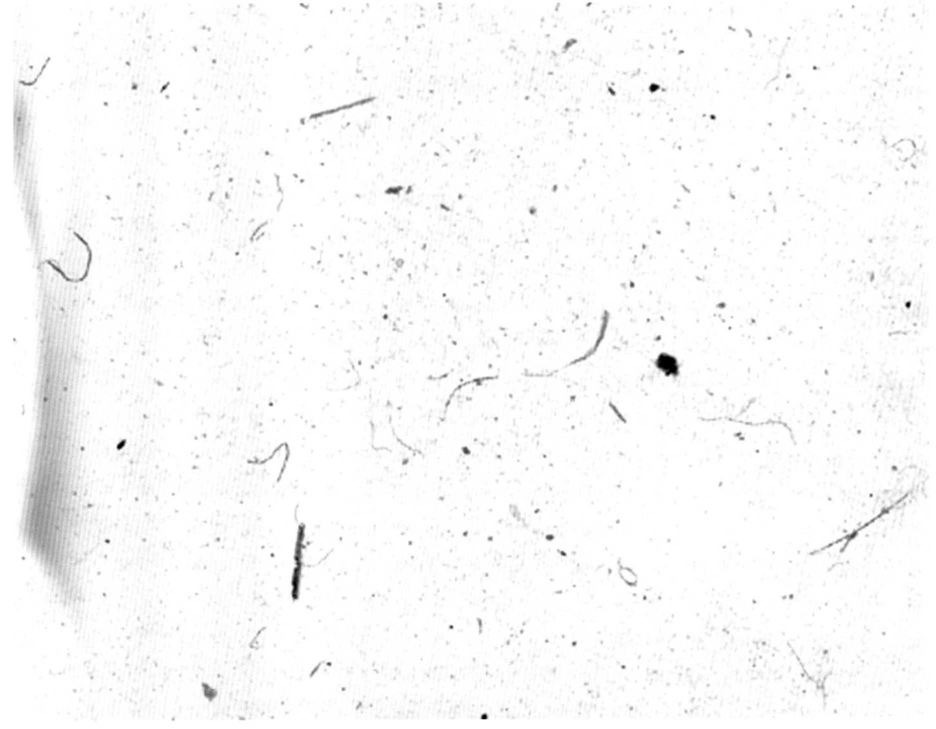

ABOVE: *Staub series 4*, pencil on inkjet photographic print, 100 x 200cm
OPPOSITE: *Gefallener, Staub IV*, pencil on gesso coated copper, 10 x 15cm

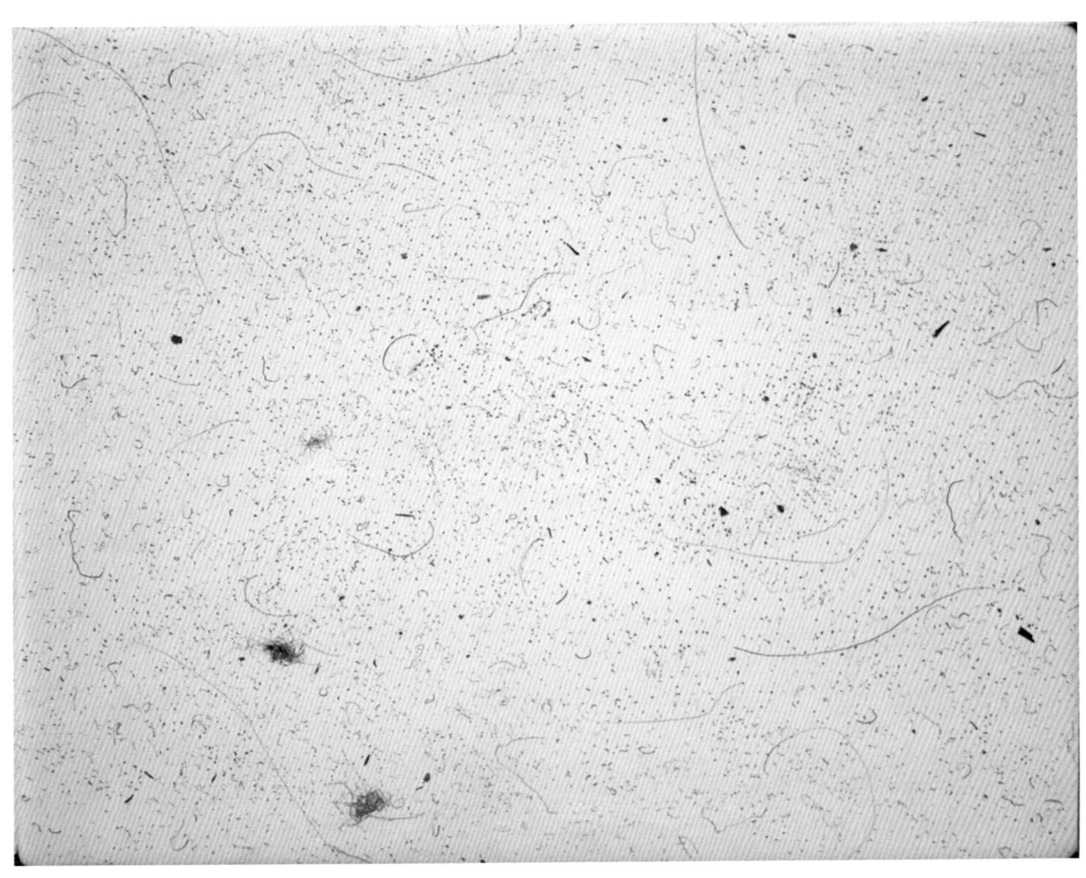

RACHEL SHARP

Portrait Painting in the Digital Age

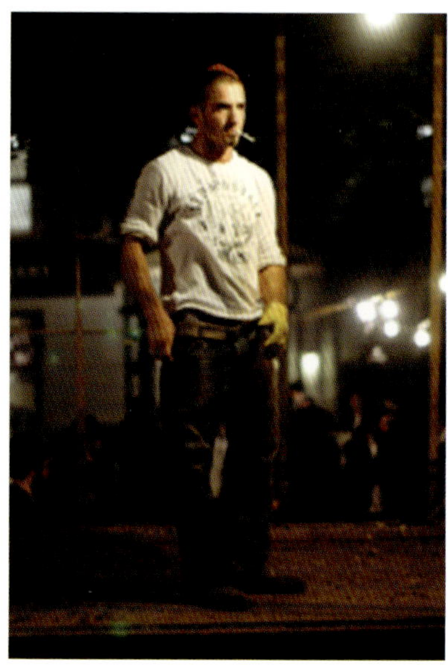

Self Portrait, Googling (2006), a painting by Dana Schutz, shows the artist sitting at a computer in her paint-spattered studio, searching for images online. In *Frieze Magazine,* Steven Stern reflects on the painting: "Schutz's work seems to be most urgently wrapped up in asking what painting is, what it means to be engaged in this particular activity at this particular time. One thing it means, clearly, is to be always engaged in an Image Search—sorting through all the possible and potential subjects and styles, and deciding what is worthy of putting onto a canvas" (Stern, online).

The fact that Schutz's paintings are primarily figurative highlights how pictures of people account for a significant part of the overwhelming quantity of images available on the Internet. As a figurative painter, my practice has developed alongside this phenomenon. My work draws upon my early training at the New York Studio School for Drawing, Painting and Sculpture. However, now, instead of working from the model, l paint from images sourced online.

What does the Digital Age mean for portrait painting? To answer this question it is useful to consider the historical evolution of the genre. A traditional source of value in portraiture is the artist's skill in conveying the subject's 'essence' or character. Thomas Gainsborough was celebrated for this ability. Furthermore, the National Portrait

Gallery was founded on the idea that paintings could connect viewers with illustrious figures from the past.

Eilean Hooper-Greenhill explains: "the portrait as a material artefact once occupied the same historical space as the sitter which it represents, and it thereby acted in a metaphysical way to bring the sitter and the present-day viewer into an almost personal contact" (2000: 39). The fixation on intimate connection has a striking parallel in the modern-day. On websites like Facebook and Twitter, users are able to 'follow' their favourite celebrities by accessing pictures and details of their daily lives.

In the nineteenth century, photography threatened to replace painting in its ability to deliver a 'close and personal' view of the subject. However, although the mechanics of the camera could usually be depended on to convey a like-ness, the ambiguous nature of representation remained. John Gage writes that a London street photographer in the 1850s managed to "fob off customers in a hurry with ready-prepared images of other people… the 'mechanical' process and some persuasive patter could thus make a young woman enthusiastically accept the photograph of an old widow as a likeness of herself, and a sailor that of a carpenter" (Woodall 1997: 120).

With the advent of mass media, portrait

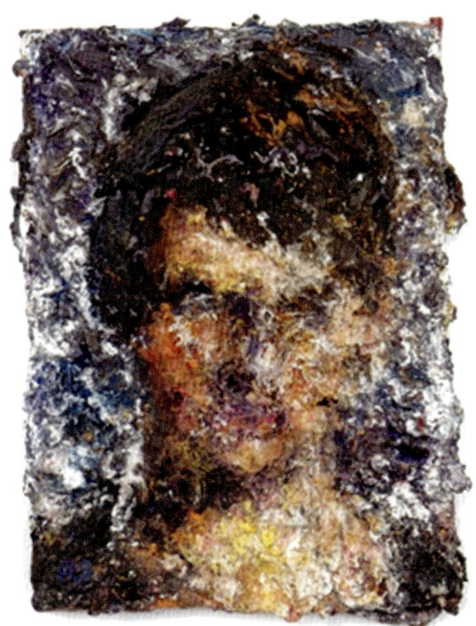

RIGHT: *Tanja Series III*, acrylic and tempera on canvas, 18 x 13cm
OPPOSITE: *New Yorker Series III* (Photograph courtesy of Brandon Stanton, Humans of New York)

painting became increasingly disconnected from the objective to reflect the subject's inner self. This is illuminated in Andy Warhol's iconic silkscreen prints of Marilyn Monroe, which redefine the portrait as a commodity. Similarly, Gerhard Richter's paintings based on mass media photographs express his view that "a portrait must not express anything of the sitter's 'soul', essence or character" (Gronert 2006: 209).

The expression of identity, whether embraced or rejected, has been linked to portrait painting throughout its history, and my own work explores how the Internet and digital media impacts upon this issue. Taking part in *Fade Away*, a 2011 exhibition at Gallery North in Newcastle upon Tyne, provided valuable insight. In this survey show of forty painters, figures were depicted morphing into objects, dissolving into fields of colour and surrounded by appropriated images from print and digital sources.

Barry Schwabsky writes in his introduction to the exhibition: "there is a tremendous interest today in what the art historian Dario Gamboni has called 'potential images', that is, those established—in the realm of the virtual—by the artist but dependent on the beholder for their realization, and their property is to make the beholder aware—either painfully or enjoyably—of the active, subjective, nature of seeing" (Sharma 2011: 77).

The close interaction between the viewer and the image, which Schwabsky describes, is mirrored in my practice. The technology in my studio— the laptop, Internet, image editing software and printer—enable a close and physical engagement with digital content. Images are easily accessed, edited and reproduced, and this manipulation carries over into painting. This is evident in the *Tanja* series of paintings, based on a single image sourced from the Internet.

The unique aesthetic qualities of digital pictures also affect my process. As Andrew Darley observes, computer-generated images lack traditional depth cues (2000: 124). The figure and ground merge together like flat puzzle pieces with little or no illusion of three-dimensional space. The absence of defined edges influences the application of paint, which is allowed to seep over the edges of the canvas. In the painting, as in the digital image, the action is concentrated in the surface, an approach which takes inspiration from Fiona Rae.

The 'picture window' is a construct which may have been abandoned long ago; however, the digital image, by virtue of its striking immateriality, elicits a yearning for a highly material approach to painting. The picture is imagined not as a window, but as a door. The tactility of painting as a counterpoint to the immaterial digital image is a central dynamic in my recent work.

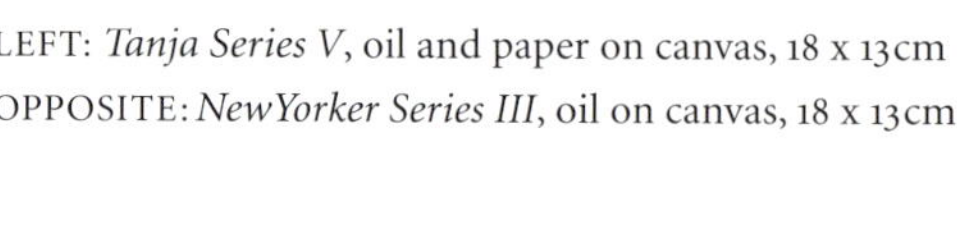

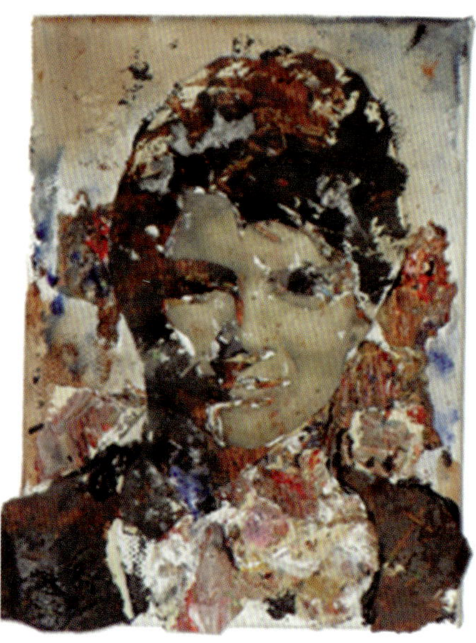

The *New Yorker* series of paintings is based, with permission, on images sourced from the *Humans of New York* Facebook page. Created by the street photographer Brandon Stanton, the page has over 600,000 followers (Stanton, online). In my paintings based on Stanton's photographs, colours are closely replicated in heavy pigment. This provides an opportunity to explore just what 'thick paint' means within the context of our digital world.

Heavily painted portraits have associations with the work of Frank Auerbach, an artist whose practice is rooted firmly in painting from the model. His canvases are completed in prolonged series of sittings which may span months or even years. Auerbach's approach, designed to develop a profound knowledge of his subjects, contrasts strongly to my method of painting images of strangers from Facebook. In my work, the physicality of the paint is less an exploration of a person than the mechanical processes of digital media. The constant manipulation of technology to mobilize, alter and reproduce images is a part of the painting process and modern life. The dark side of this busy engagement with technology is that it risks being perpetual and meaningless.

In the short film, *On Handwork*, the textile artist Renate Hiller expresses concern over the loss of tactile senses in our computer dominated environment. She comments: "To have the skill of the use of the hands is vital for a human being for having flexibility and dexterity… and what do we do in our modern world with the hands? We move the mouse, we drive, we feel plastic most of the time" (Hiller, online). Painting is both a reflection and a remedy for this condition. The material experience of the pigment, applied slowly by hand, seeks to fill the emptiness of digital interaction. In this sense, my paintings are portraits of the human experience of the Digital Age.

References

DARLEY, A. (2000) *Visual Digital Culture: Surface Play and Spectacle in New Media Genres*, London: Routledge

GRONERT, S. (2006) *Gerhard Richter: Portraits*, Ostfildern: Hatje Cantz Verlag

HILLER, R. 'On Painting', cited at http://www.onbeing.org/blog/world-through-hands/3931, accessed 20/02/2013

HOOPER-GREENHILL, E. (2000) *Museums and the Interpretation of Visual Culture*, London: Routledge

SHARMA, A. (2011) *About Painting*, London: Transition Editions

STANTON, B. 'Humans of New York', cited at www.humansofnewyork.com, accessed 06/02/2013

STERN, S. 'Image Search', cited at http://www.frieze.com/issue/print_article/image_search, accessed 15/01/2013

WOODALL, J. (Ed.) (1997) *Portraiture: Facing the Subject*, Manchester: Manchester University Press

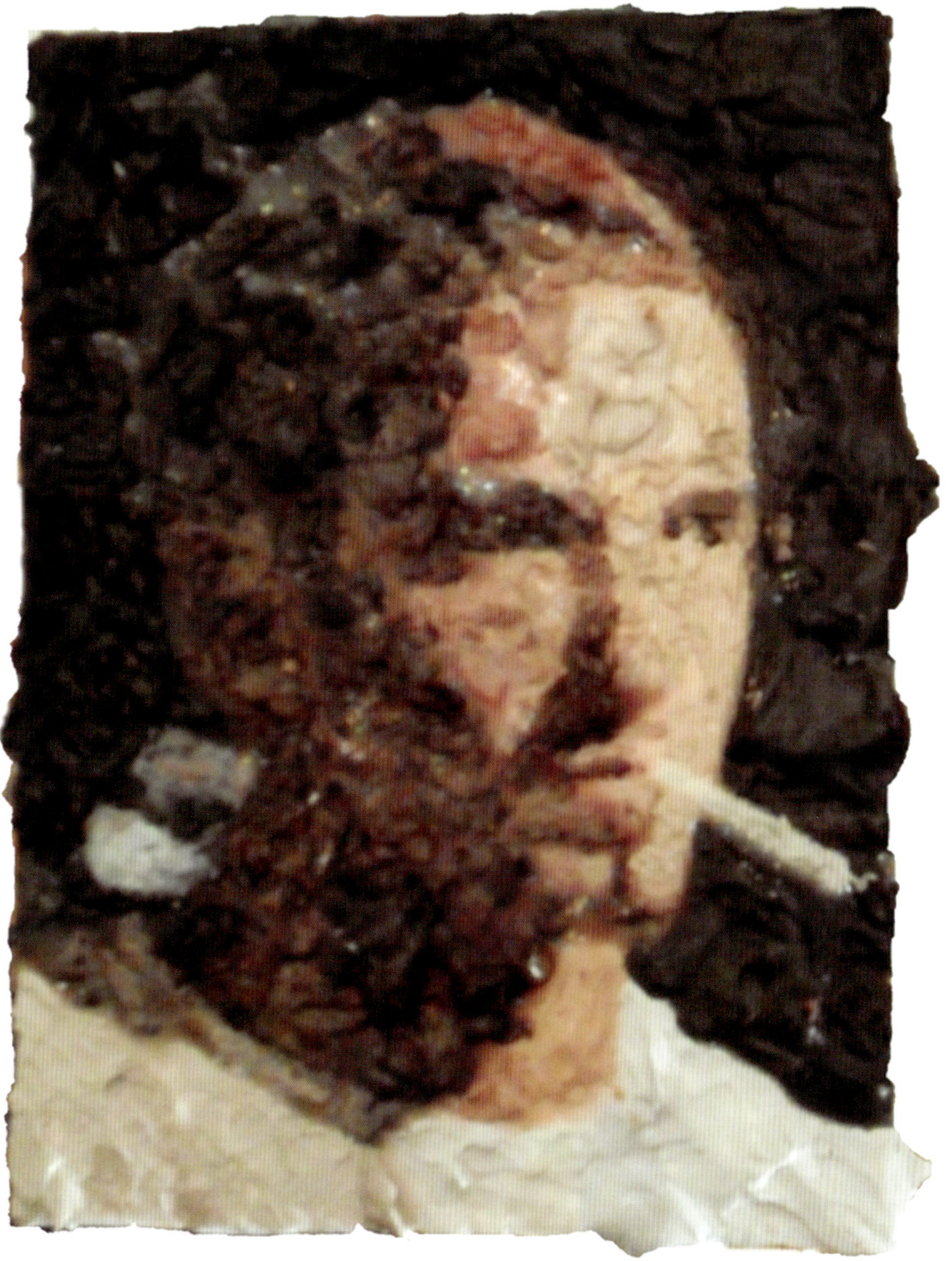